The genius of marketing

"Marketing is not the art of finding clever ways to dispose of what you make. It is the art of creating genuine customer value."

Philip Kotler

Praise for this book

"Nobody covers marketing like Kotler. The range and depth of his knowledge is enormous. Everyone, even a marketing expert, can benefit from reading his comprehensive new book."

Al Ries, co-author, *The Origin of Brands*

"Kotler proves, once again, his own renovation of thought keeps him current and required reading for today's executive."

Sergio Zyman, chairman and founder, The Zyman Group

Praise for the author

"If you want to learn marketing, you have to come to Kotler. He is both a pioneer of modern marketing and the leading popularizer of the field."

Publishers Weekly

"He may have led the marketing debate for over thirty years yet there is no sign of Kotler resting on his laurels. He keeps up to speed with current marketing trends and recently conducted research into the new economy and the effect of the Internet on marketing."

From *www.thinkers50.co.uk*, a website of the world's top 50 business thinkers

PHILIP KOTLER is one of the world's foremost experts on strategic marketing, and was voted the first Leader in Marketing Thought by the American Marketing Association. He is currently the S. C. Johnson & Son Distinguished Professor of International Marketing at the Kellogg School of Management of Northwestern University in Chicago. His many influential books have sold more than three million copies in 20 languages, and include *Marketing Management* (now in its twelfth edition) and *Kotler on Marketing*. He lives in Evanston, Illinois.

02871

This book is due for return on or before the last date shown below.

Business

Copyright © 2008 Philip Kotler

Paperback edition published in 2008 by:

Marshall Cavendish Limited
Fifth Floor
32–38 Saffron Hill
London EC1N 8FH
United Kingdom
T: +44 (0)20 7421 8120
F: +44 (0)20 7421 8121
sales@marshallcavendish.co.uk
www.marshallcavendish.co.uk

First published in North America by AMACOM, a division of
American Management Association, New York in 2005

This edition is not for sale in North America

The right of Philip Kotler to be identified as the author of this work has been
asserted by him in accordance with the Copyright, Designs and Patents Act 1988.

A CIP record for this book is available from the British Library

ISBN 978-1-905736-49-2

Printed and bound in Great Britain by
CPI Bookmarque, Croydon CR0 4TD

Contents

Preface

Over the years, I have received thousands of questions about marketing from clients, students, business audiences, and journalists. Certain questions came up repeatedly. I found that these questions varied in quality. Some were brilliant questions and made me think freshly about an answer. Some were naïve questions, but even these often stimulated new thoughts.

One of my colleagues suggested that because these questions come up all the time, I might consider putting them together in book form. In this way, marketers who have the same questions but have never had a chance to ask them could satisfy their curiosity.

I faced the difficult task of figuring out how to sequence numerous questions on a great variety of subjects. I rejected the idea of listing the questions randomly. Instead, I arranged the questions according to a set of logical topics to make it easy for the readers to indulge their curiosity selectively.

Thus we start with a look at questions about markets and marketing. Following this, we comment on the main ideas in marketing strategy (segmentation, targeting, positioning, and differentiation). Next, we answer questions about the main tools of marketing, known as the 4Ps (product, price, place, and promotion). Marketing planning comes next, followed by marketing organization and marketing control. We then answer questions about many areas of marketing application—consumer packaged goods, retail marketing, small-business marketing, direct marketing, Internet marketing, professional service marketing, personal marketing, international marketing, place marketing, recession marketing, political marketing, and social responsibility marketing. As a grand finale, we comment on marketing excellence as practiced by the best companies.

Although the questions are sequenced according to this outline, the reader will have no trouble looking up questions and answers that relate to any specific marketing topic of interest. The book includes a detailed index listing every topic that has been discussed. If the reader does not find a question on a particular marketing topic of interest, the reason is that no one has asked me that question.

There is a good chance that readers will disagree with some of my answers. I welcome disagreement because that is the way we can collectively improve our understanding of marketing.

My answers are rarely long, and many questions deserve more extended commentary. But I felt that readers who are driven by curiosity about my answers should go to any of the many books that treat the respective subjects more deeply.

I was going to title the book *Everything You Always Wanted to Ask about Marketing but Were Afraid to Ask*. Then I thought that a shorter title would do.

Bon voyage!

FAQs on

MARKETING

PART 1

Markets and Marketing

Definition

What is marketing?

Marketing is the science and art of exploring, creating, and delivering value to satisfy the needs of a target market at a profit. Marketing identifies unfulfilled needs and desires. It defines, measures, and quantifies the size of the identified market and its profit potential. It pinpoints the market segments that the company is capable of serving best, and it designs and promotes the appropriate products and services.

Marketing is often performed by a department within the organization. This is both good and bad. It's good because it brings together a group of trained people who focus on the marketing task. It's bad because marketing activities should not be carried out in a single department—they should be manifest in all the activities of the organization.

In your opinion, what are the main concepts used in marketing?

The most important concepts used in marketing are segmentation, targeting, positioning, needs, wants, demand, offerings, brands, value and satisfaction, exchange, transactions, relationships and networks, marketing channels, supply chain, competition, the marketing environment, and marketing programs. These terms, which I describe in the eleventh edition of my book *Marketing Management,* make up the working vocabulary of the marketing professional.

How would you summarize the key processes involved in marketing and their importance?

The key processes in marketing are (1) opportunity identification, (2) new product development, (3) customer attraction, (4) customer retention and loyalty building, and (5) order fulfillment. A company that handles all of these processes well will normally enjoy success. But when a company fails at *any one* of these processes, it will do poorly.

Many companies see marketing as mainly a department, but you've described it as a total company philosophy and practice. How is that?

Many years ago, David Packard, who co-created Hewlett-Packard, said, "Marketing is far too important to leave to the marketing department." A company can have the best marketing department in the world and still fail at marketing. Why? Because the manufacturing people may put out poor-quality products, the shipping department may ship late, the accounting department may send out inaccurate invoices . . . all of which will lose customers. Marketing is effective only if the whole company delivers the promised value and satisfies the customer.

Doesn't marketing have to be adapted to each country and region? Are there any fixed principles?

Marketing is not a fixed subject like analytic geometry. And marketing should not be practiced in the same way in different countries that have different economies, cultures, and politics. Even within a country, marketing should be practiced differently in consumer goods industries, business-to-business industries, and service industries. Different companies within the same industry will be found to practice marketing differently. All effective marketing is local.

Nonetheless, there are certain marketing principles that are fairly constant. Among them are:

- Respect the centrality of customers, competitors, and distributors in the planning of marketing strategy.
- Apply segmentation to every market and go after the segments that are most promising in terms of your company's capabilities and goals.
- For each target market segment, research the needs, perceptions, preferences, and buying processes of the customers.
- Win by carefully defining, creating, and delivering a superior value promise to the target market.

I know that anyone's theory on any subject may become obsolete. Copernicus replaced Ptolemy and Einstein replaced Copernicus in understanding the universe. As soon as I see signs of a radically new and better marketing theory, I will be the first to adopt it.

What are some of the chief misconceptions about effective marketing that are still operating in today's companies? Who isn't "getting it?"

Marketing is a terribly misunderstood subject in business circles and in the public's mind. Companies think that marketing exists to support manufacturing, to get rid of the company's products. The truth is the reverse: Manufacturing exists to support marketing. The company can always outsource its manufacturing. What makes a company is its marketing offerings and ideas. Manufacturing, purchasing, R&D, finance, and the other company functions exist to help the company achieve its goals in the customer marketplace.

Marketing is too often confused with selling. Selling is only the tip of the marketing iceberg. What is unseen is the extensive market investigation, the research and development of appropriate products, and the challenge of pricing them right, of opening up distribution, and of letting the market know about the product. Thus, marketing is a far more comprehensive process than selling.

Marketing and selling are almost opposites. Hard-sell marketing is a contradiction. Long ago I said: "Marketing is not the art of finding clever ways to dispose of what you make. Marketing is the art of creating genuine customer value. It is the art of helping your customers become better off. The marketer's watchwords are quality, service, and value."

Selling starts only when you have a product. Marketing starts before there is a product. Marketing is the homework that the company does to figure out what people need and what the company should make. Marketing determines how to launch, price, distribute, and promote the product or service offering in the marketplace. Marketing then monitors the results and improves the offering over time. Marketing also decides when to change or drop the offering.

With all that said, marketing is not a short-term selling effort but a long-term investment effort. When marketing is done well, it occurs before the company makes any product or enters any market; and it continues long after the sale.

When did marketing first appear?

Marketing started with the first human beings. Using the first Bible story as an example, we see Eve convincing Adam to eat the forbidden apple. But Eve was not the first marketer. It was the snake that convinced her to market to Adam.

Marketing as a topic appeared in the United States in the first part of the twentieth century in the teaching of courses having to do with distribution, particularly wholesaling and retailing. Economists, in their passion for pure theory, had neglected the institutions that help an economy function. Demand and supply curves show where price may settle but do not explain the chain of prices all the way from the manufacturer through the wholesalers through the retailers. So early marketers filled in the intellectual gaps left by economists. Nevertheless, economics is the mother science of marketing. Many of us are essentially "market economists."

Is marketing more an art or a craft?

Marketing is more of a craft and a profession than an art form. The American Marketing Association and the British Chartered Institute of Marketing are independently working on professional credentials for marketers. They believe that tests can be constructed that can distinguish between qualified marketers and phony marketers.

At the same time, many people who are not trained marketers will originate brilliant marketing ideas. Ingvar Kamprad was not a marketer, and yet his IKEA company is phenomenally successful in bringing good-quality, low-cost furniture to the masses. Creativity is a big part of marketing success and is not limited to marketers.

But science is also important to marketing. Marketers produce interesting findings through market research, market modeling, and predictive analytics. Marketers are using marketing models to make decisions and guide their investments. They are developing marketing metrics to capture the impact of their activities on sales and profits.

I would not say that marketing is more of an art, a craft, or a science, but rather that all these elements are operating.

Is marketing an applied science?

Just as engineering draws its strengths from basic disciplines such as physics and chemistry, the marketing discipline draws its strengths from several basic disciplines, such as economics, psychology, sociology, organizational theory, mathematics, and decision science. As these basic sciences advance, so will marketing. I believe that marketing will eventually be transmuted into the science of demand management and will develop more comprehensive theories of what drives demand and how to optimize profits.

When did marketing start to include concepts from psychology, sociology, and anthropology, as well as from economics?

Marketers eventually realized that buyers, not sellers, are at the center of the marketing universe. To understand buyers, it is necessary for marketers to study the behavioral and organizational sciences. Marketing researchers must use their knowledge of demography, psychology, culture, and social influence to understand customer needs, perceptions, preferences, and behaviors, in order to develop more effective marketing strategies.

The use of the term *marketing* is now expanding beyond the area of ordinary goods and services. Is this good?

I share a lot of the responsibility for the broadened use of the term *marketing*. In 1969, Sidney Levy and I wrote an article called "Broadening the Concept of Marketing." We claimed that marketing can be used not only by profit-making organizations but also by nonprofit organizations such as museums, churches, charities, and so on that want to attract clients, volunteers, and funds. We further argued that marketing can be applied to the launch of social campaigns such as "don't smoke," "don't use hard drugs," "eat healthy foods," "exercise daily," "don't litter," and many other such causes.

Today I go further and argue that we can market goods, services, experiences, information, property, places, persons, organizations, and causes. Like any concept, marketing can be used for good or bad purposes. I maintain that applying a marketing mindset generally does much more good than harm.

Is it possible that the products available today meet all or almost all of our needs and that the problem facing marketing is that there are few remaining needs to be met?

In marketing, we always talk about meeting unfulfilled needs. At present, there are an abundance of products to meet most needs. My friend Pietro Guido from Italy wrote a book entitled *The No Need Society* in order to advance the argument that marketers must learn how to create needs, much as Sony does with new electronic equipment. Many years ago, who needed Walkmen, huge TV screens, or tiny videocameras? Companies should shift from being market driven (driven by consumers' needs) to being market driving (aimed at creating new markets).

At the same time, there are always unfulfilled needs. The person who works hard will crave a vacation; later, he will crave going back to work. Also, every newborn child will represent a new bundle of unfulfilled needs.

Why is marketing the best way to satisfy individual needs?

People can try to satisfy their needs in many ways, including stealing or begging. The marketing way of satisfying needs is to offer something of value in exchange for what one wants from the other party. The basic concept of marketing is exchange. It is the most reasonable and voluntary way for people to acquire goods in a civilized society.

Is marketing the same in the consumer goods, services, and business-to-business areas?

Many marketing ideas and tools originally evolved out of problems faced by fast-moving consumer packaged goods companies. Other tools evolved out of durable goods industries (both consumer and industrial), commodity industries, and service industries. The marketing framework of STP (segmentation, targeting, and positioning) and the 4Ps (product, price, place, and promotion) helps us analyze and plan for any market, whether for a product or a service. Each market, of course, has its special characteristics, and additional ideas and tools are usually required. Service marketers, for example, pay heavy attention to three more Ps (personnel, process, and physical evidence) in developing their marketing plans. In no way, however, do I think that each type of market (consumer, industrial, and service) needs an entirely new and different framework. Otherwise, we would have to talk about Marketing Type 1, Marketing Type 2, and Marketing Type 3 and would believe that no industry can learn from another industry.

What is the mission of marketing?

At least three different answers have been given to this question. The earliest answer was that the mission of marketing is to sell any and all of the company's products to anyone and everyone. A second, more sophisticated answer is that the mission of marketing is to create products that satisfy the well-defined needs of well-defined target markets. A third, more philosophical answer is that the mission of marketing is to raise the material standard of living and the quality of life throughout the world.

Marketing's role is to sense people's unfulfilled needs and create new and attractive solutions. The modern kitchen and its equipment provide a fine example, liberating women from tedious housework so that they have time to develop their higher capacities.

You say that marketing must play the lead role in shaping business strategy. Do you think that business executives are fully aware of the role that marketing can play in helping the company succeed?

Some CEOs see marketing as a department that comes into play after the product has been made and the remaining job is to sell it. We argue instead that marketing must drive the strategy for each business unit. It must be the starting point in developing the business plan. Peter Drucker stated it well over thirty years ago: "A company has only two basic functions: innovation and marketing."

You have said that if the people in a company's marketing department can't propose any new opportunities, they should be fired. But are there many good opportunities still left?

Granted, the absolute number of opportunities in an economy will vary with the business cycle and the technology cycle and the speed of globalization. Opportunities will be scarcer during recessions and when new technologies have not yet emerged and when trade barriers exist.

But there are always opportunities! Just look at the new products that continue to appear in catalogs such as *Sharper Image* or *Innovation* or *Fascination*. Any company with a product or service should be able to think of new ways to modify it, combine it, offer different sizes, or add new features or services.

Not only can an offering be reshaped for different markets, but the offering can also be visualized in a new context.

I published *Lateral Marketing* (with coauthor Fernando Trias De Bes), which offers a creativity approach that differs from vertical marketing (i.e., segmentation) for finding new ideas. Vertical marketing works within a given market; lateral marketing instead visualizes the product in a new context. Many examples can be cited. Today we can buy food at gas stations; we can do our banking in a supermarket; we can get access to a computer at cybercafes; we can take pictures with a cell phone; we can chew medical gum to ingest certain medicines; we can eat cereal in the form of a candy bar. I can't believe there aren't opportunities. I can believe only that some marketers lack the ability to see opportunities. Marketing doesn't have to fail during a recession; only marketers who lack an imagination fail.

What significant business opportunities do you identify in the evolving economy?

Here is my list of significant business opportunities:

- Biotech (e.g., individualized drug design, biometric measurement for security)
- Mobile phones (e.g., micropayments through the phone; instant news; text messaging)
- Security (corporate and home security)

- Niche businesses (e.g., a bank for Latinos; a children's bookstore)
- Automation (e.g., fast-passing through toll gates)
- Health care (new medical devices; drugs; lifestyle changes; alternative therapies)
- Robots (for production, housecleaning, lawn care, military combat)
- Outsourcing
- Storage systems

Ask the following questions:

1. Is there a substantial market?
2. What is the competitive landscape?
3. Can you develop a profitable business model?
4. Can you scale up quickly?

What is the difference between marketing and merchandising?

Merchandising is a term that is used mostly in retailing to describe the retailer's selection of goods to display in the store and the best ways to display the goods. Marketing is a much broader term of which merchandising is only one activity.

What are the most logical telltale signs that you need to do something about your marketing—aside from declining sales?

Here are other telltale signs:

1. Sales are flat and the company needs a growth strategy.

2. Sales pass through high and low seasons that need to be leveled.
3. Sales are okay, but margins are too low.
4. The profits from certain products, customer segments, or distribution channels are too low.

How about this: Where does the CEO or business owner who really isn't that savvy about marketing begin—aside from reading your books?

Actually, I would propose that one of my books would constitute the best starting point—not my 700-page *Marketing Management* (eleventh edition), but my 270-page *Kotler on Marketing*. It lays out the basic concepts, principles, and strategies. For readers looking for marketing tips, especially for small businesses, Jay Conrad Levinson's book *Guerrilla Marketing* would be useful to read. Finally, there are many books dealing with particular marketing subjects, such as building brands, managing communications, setting prices, working with intermediaries, and developing an effective sales force.

How has marketing changed since its beginnings?

Marketing had its start as a subject that broke away from economics. Early marketers focused on trying to understand distribution channels. Most economists showed demand and supply curves determining a market price without looking at different levels of distribution. Early marketing was descriptive and institutional. In addition to channels, early marketing focused on advertising and personal selling. Many people began to think of marketing as a fancier word for selling. It took many years for marketing to liberate itself from being seen this way. Here are the main stages in marketing's evolution:

- The 4Ps marked a step forward because this concept identified product, price, place, and promotion as the constituent decisions in preparing a market offering. Marketers later realized that in order to set the 4Ps, they needed to understand customers better and moved to the 4Cs—customer value, customer costs, customer convenience, and customer communication.
- Marketers later introduced the notion that the 4Ps should be preceded by STP strategic thinking: segmentation, targeting, and positioning.
- Marketers then realized that a company can operate on four targeting levels: the mass market, a market segment, a market niche, or an individual customer.
- Marketing later was generalized into the skill set of managing the level, timing, and composition of demand.
- Marketing was further broadened to including the marketing not only of products and services but also of ideas, causes, places, people, organizations, and other entities.

Do marketing theory and practice change very much?

Recently the CEO of a large company asked me to sign a copy of my first edition (1967) of *Marketing Management,* on which his marketing education had been based. I refused, saying that the first edition of *Marketing Management* was useless. In 1967, we knew little about segmentation; we had never heard of positioning; branding was a minor subject; we did not know about the brilliant strategies of Wal-Mart, Southwest Airlines, and IKEA; the Internet, cell phones, and PDAs did not exist; and so on. I said that the eleventh edition of *Marketing Management,* published in 2003, is a hundred times more useful than the first edition. He said, "Are you trying to sell me a new book?" "Of course," I said, "but because it will give you more value." Then I relented and signed his relic, having made my point that markets change and, therefore, marketing has to change.

If you were forming a business and building a sales and marketing infrastructure, if you had your pick between a great salesman or a great marketing man—and you could afford only one—which would you pick? Why?

For short-run results, I would choose the great salesman. But for long-run success, I would choose the great marketing man. Sales is all about disposing of the present products being made by the company. But it doesn't answer what products the company should be making in the first place.

What is the worst type of marketing?

Marketing is essentially a philosophy that emphasizes the importance of understanding, serving, and satisfying customer needs. Practices such as bait and switch, exaggerated advertising, and deceptive pricing undercut the marketing concept.

Is there anything particularly encouraging in marketing today that makes you personally feel optimistic about its future?

Today's marketers are better trained than ever. In the past, marketers got their training from selling on the street and moved into marketing positions later. Their formal marketing education was weak at best. Today we are training marketers to be more financially competent and to use more financial metrics in measuring the impact of their marketing expenditures on profit. At the same time, we are giving them more tools for market analysis, market segmentation, strategy simulation, and database mining.

In your definition of "demarketing," you suggest that marketing can be used to dissuade people from using certain products and services. Doesn't that annul the marketing concept, which is "to meet customers' needs?"

I don't believe in the indiscriminant satisfying of all customers' needs because there are other considerations that may play a role. Thus, if a community is experiencing a water shortage, the demand must be reduced either by marketing efforts or by legal efforts. Marketing is a set of tools that can be used to adjust the level, timing, and composition of demand to meet the organization's or society's objectives. Demarketing describes the use of marketing tools to cool demand, as opposed to heating it up.

What are some major characteristics of recent U.S. marketing?

- U.S. companies are doing more outsourcing. They are becoming more virtual companies.
- U.S. companies are doing more comparison benchmarking against competitors and world-class performers and are ready to change more frequently and radically.
- U.S. companies, especially the smaller ones, are more entrepreneurial.
- U.S. companies have moved much faster into direct

marketing through catalogs, telemarketing, direct mail, and Web-based marketing.

Of course, these are generalizations, and many exceptions exist.

What have you been emphasizing in your speeches about the nature of marketing?

Many people see marketing only in its tactical form, namely, a lot of advertising and sales promotion. They see only the tip of the marketing iceberg. Strategic marketing is less visible but more potent. My aim has been to explain how the marketplace really works, to give real-life texture to the theories of the economists. My thesis is that winning companies make their customers into winners. Smart companies continuously create new value for their customers. They are thoroughly customer-centered and customer-driven.

I have also promoted the idea that marketing is a science; that marketing expenditures are partly investments; that buyer behavior can be understood and modeled; and that product features, product positioning, prices, advertising, sales promotion, services, and distribution arrangements can be modeled and optimized by disciplined marketing thinking.

How is the role of marketing changing today in the light of globalization and new technology?

Marketing as we know it—research, segmentation, targeting, positioning, and the 4Ps—must be reconceptualized as we move from a slowly changing world to a turbulent global economy. In the 1980s, we would say: "Ready, aim, fire." In the 1990s, we would say: "Ready, fire, aim." Today we are saying: "Fire, fire, fire." In the past, we used to aim for the mass market; today we can target each individual prospect. In the past, we produced a product with a fairly long life cycle; today we are more prepared to customize the product according to each buyer's wishes. In the past, we would set a price; now buyers are proposing the price. The advent of the Internet and the development of customer databases is revolutionizing marketing. Many of the concepts still apply, but we must translate their meaning in the new economy.

What are some basic things that nearly all businesses engage in that you consider marketing but that many businesspeople may not realize are marketing?

Businesses fail to realize the full extent of their marketing activities and costs. For example, the Red Lobster chain is planning to change the décor of its restaurants. This will probably appear in the books as a paint or maintenance expense. But it is actually undertaken to market better to customers. Or consider a bank that invests in an expensive customer relationship management (CRM) software system and lists it as an information technology (IT) expense. But it really is done to improve the bank's marketing effectiveness in targeting customers. Marketing is a much higher cost in today's companies than is reflected in their conventional marketing expenses.

Do you think that knowing at least some marketing concepts is essential for everybody nowadays?

Yes. I have described major concepts in marketing in my book *Marketing Insights from A to Z: 80 Concepts That Managers Need to Know.* I wrote this book for nonmarketing managers who need to understand marketing better, and for marketing managers who need to update their knowledge. In the book, I describe such concepts as segmentation, targeting, positioning, the marketing mix, distribution channels, image, quality, value, differentiation, customer relationship marketing, database marketing, and so forth. Many of these concepts apply outside of normal business management and can guide everyone's thinking and behavior.

Do you think that marketing should be taught in high schools? Why?

Yes. About ten years ago, I received a letter from a publisher in the Netherlands inviting me to write a high school textbook on marketing. The publisher said that the Dutch people are traders by nature and depend on understanding other cultures and how to exchange value. He thought that marketing would be more interesting to high school students than economics, or would at least breathe life into economics. The reason is that students confront marketing all the time: in TV commercials, in retail stores, in the music industry, in contests, and so on. They would enjoy the stories of competitors such as Coca-Cola vs. Pepsi Cola or McDonald's vs. Burger King, and the course would shed light on their everyday lives and also prove useful in their working lives. But I decided not to write the book.

Regis McKenna wrote an article in the *Harvard Business Review* with the title "Marketing Is Everything." Do you agree?

Regis McKenna wrote a stimulating article. But when something is everything, it is nothing. My concept of customer-centered marketing is different. Customer-centered marketing calls for everyone in an organization to wear a "marketing hat" as part of the total business wardrobe. Thus a company's financial vice president, when she is seeking a bank loan, will be more effective if she thinks of the bank's needs and concerns as she prepares her case for the loan. Each person in an organization engages in exchange situations, and marketing offers the tools for managing exchange situations effectively.

What is holistic marketing? How does it differ from traditional marketing? Could you briefly explain how holistic marketing can enable companies to design winning market offerings?

Holistic marketing is essentially a move from a product focus to a customer focus, from selling products to satisfying customers. This has been going on for a while and is getting stronger.

Holistic marketing calls for the company to implement four processes:

- Enlarge its view of its customers' needs and lifestyles. The company should stop seeing its customers only as consumers of its current products and start visualizing broader ways to serve them and their lifestyles.
- Assess how all of its departments affect customer satisfaction. Customers are adversely affected when their products arrive late or are damaged, when invoices are inaccurate, when customer service is poor, or when other foul-ups occur. Marketing's task is to unify everyone in the company to "think customer" and deliver the company's brand promise.
- Assess the impact of its actions on all the company's stakeholders—customers, employees, distributors, dealers, and suppliers, not just its shareholders. Any alienated stakeholder group can create havoc with the

company's plans and progress. Holistic marketing calls for partnering with the employees, suppliers, and distributors to work as a team to deliver the best value to the target customers.

• Take a larger view of the company's industry—its players and its evolution. Today many industries are converging, presenting new opportunities and new threats to each industry player.

Holistic marketing is a step in changing the company's architecture to implement the concept of the customer collaborating with the company and even driving the company. Marketing cannot work unless it is holistic.

Customer Power and Satisfaction

Power has shifted from the suppliers to the customers. Why?

The growing proliferation of products and competitors means that there is not a shortage of products, there is a shortage of customers. This makes the customer king. The customer has more choice than ever before, and also more information, thanks to the Internet. The customer can click on "shopping bots" such as buy.com or mysimon.com that show the prices charged by different online merchants for the same item. Prices can vary as much as 20 percent. The consumer is only a click away from checking different suppliers, which is not the case when doing store shopping. Consumers can also chat with owners or users of the product, which means that word of mouth will grow more important in influencing consumer choice.

Suppliers will have to be more careful. Their offerings

will be under a microscope. Their costs cannot be far out of line. High-cost suppliers will lose out. The Internet will lead to falling prices and margins, and to a Darwinian survival of the fittest.

Companies say that "the customer is number one." Isn't this a good sign that companies are becoming market-oriented?

Most companies describe themselves as customer-oriented, but few practice this. The managing director often makes speeches about the importance of customer focus. However, the message doesn't sink into the minds of middle and lower management because there are many other demands on their time and they are measured by quite different performance criteria.

Companies that are experiencing a strong demand for their products and services have to avoid becoming less responsive. I know one leading investment company whose analysts act like prima donnas, answering phone calls late, keeping customers waiting, and showing benign neglect. Predictably, a competitor with a superior reputation for customer care has emerged who is now taking market share away from the leader.

"The customer is number one" is more talk than reality. Customer care attitudes must be implemented, not merely talked about. A company that is serious about making the customer number one must take several steps. It must track the level of customer satisfaction in relation to competitors' levels of customer satisfaction. It must develop maps showing all the points of interaction between its personnel and its customers, especially noting points of customer breakdown or disappointment. And it must introduce a strong training program to cultivate positive staff attitudes, one involving critical incidents and role playing.

What are reverse marketing, reverse pricing, reverse advertising, reverse distribution, and reverse design?

"Reverse marketing" comes from the observation that customers are taking a more active role in influencing a company's product, price, place, and promotion. They are increasingly participating in designing the products they want from companies (reverse design). Examples are computers from Dell Computer and jeans from Levi's. More customers today are telling suppliers what price they will pay for an air trip, hotel, or car; the site priceline.com is an example (reverse pricing). Customers are more insistent on advertisers asking for their permission before sending ads, promotions, and offers (reverse advertising). And customers want a choice of distribution channels—in the case of a bank, for example, a teller, an automatic teller machine, a phone call, or home banking (reverse distribution). So reverse marketing describes the buyer taking more initiative in defining the terms of exchange.

I'm not sure what a "prosumer" is. Can you elaborate?

Some companies create an environment in which they act as workshops from which the customers create the products and services they want. Dell offers a perfect example in that the consumer designs the product he wants. To that extent, Dell's customers are acting as prosumers (i.e., producing consumers) rather than passive consumers.

What do you think are the most important factors in creating customer satisfaction these days?

Customers are most concerned with quality, service, and value. All of these constitute competitive opportunities in markets where they are lacking. However, we are noticing that many companies and industries are rapidly improving their quality, service, and value. Consequently, these benefits are becoming normal expectations rather than distinctive winning attributes. Now design, speed, and customization are becoming more critical in influencing customer choice. Depending on the industry and product type, market leaders will find further attributes and benefits that they can turn into salient and compelling differentiators.

Trends in Marketing

Which megatrends do we have to consider for the future?

The economic landscape has been fundamentally altered by technology and globalization. Companies anywhere can now compete anywhere, thanks to the Internet and more free trade.

The major economic force is hypercompetition; namely, companies are able to produce more goods than can be sold, putting a lot of pressure on price. This also drives companies to build in more differentiation. However, a lot of the differentiation is psychological, not real. Even then, a company's current advantage doesn't last very long in an economy where any advantage can be copied rapidly.

Companies must pay attention to the fact that customers are getting more educated and have better tools, such as the Internet, at their disposal and thus can buy with more discrimination.

In your books, you have pointed out that globalization, hypercompetition, and the Internet are reshaping markets and businesses. What effect are these dynamics having on marketing?

All three forces act to increase downward pressure on prices. Globalization means that companies will move their production to cheaper sites and bring products into a country at prices lower than those charged by the domestic sellers. Hypercompetition means that there are more suppliers competing for the same customer, leading to price cuts. And the Internet means that people can compare prices more quickly and move to the lowest-cost offer. The marketing challenge, then, is to find ways to maintain prices and profitability in the face of these macro trends. No country's industry is going to hold on to its customers if it can't continue to lead in offering the most value.

At the same time, various world regions are becoming more integrated and more protective. The members of a region are seeking preferential terms from the other members of the region. But artificial trade preferences cannot last long against a substantial deterioration in value.

What are the main new trends in marketing?

My list would include:

- From make-and-sell marketing to sense-and-respond marketing
- From owning assets to owning brands
- From vertical integration to virtual integration (outsourcing)
- From mass marketing to customized marketing
- From operating only in the marketplace to also operating in cyberspace
- From pursuing market share to pursuing customer share
- From focusing on customer attraction to focusing on customer retention
- From transaction marketing to relationship marketing
- From customer acquisition to customer retention and satisfaction

- From mediated marketing to direct marketing
- From marketer monologue to customer dialogue
- From separated planning of communications to integrated marketing communications
- From single-channel marketing to multichannel marketing
- From product-centric marketing to customer-centric marketing
- From the marketing department doing the marketing to everyone in the company doing the marketing
- From exploiting suppliers and distributors to partnering with them

A discussion of the impact of each of these trends would be require a large amount of space. These trends will affect different industries and companies at different times. I hope that companies will monitor these trends and make sure that their business model is aligned with them.

How will organizations be affected by the substantial increase in the velocity of change?

Successful companies must practice *trend watching* and *scenario planning*. It never hurts to identify trends and speculate about their implications for the company. Companies can also benefit from imagining different future scenarios and planning responses to them. Smart firms will appoint a person or group to monitor trends and test scenarios. Royal Dutch/Shell attributes some of its profitability to the use of scenario planning.

What are the major changes within the field of marketing since the famous 4Ps?

There have been countless changes. We have been shifting from mass marketing to segment marketing to niche marketing to one-to-one marketing. We have recognized the growing importance of service. We have improved our skills at brand building and brand asset management. We are making better use of Web marketing. We are developing new metrics for measuring the impact of marketing expenditures.

New Ideas in Marketing

What are the newest skills needed in marketing?

Marketing traditionally has relied on four marketing skills and tools: the sales force, advertising, sales promotion, and marketing research. Every company needs to master these tools. But marketing departments also need a whole new set of skills. Among them are brand building, customer relationship management, database marketing and mining, telemarketing, experiential marketing, and profitability analysis by product, segment, channel, and customer.

What is experiential marketing?

Marketers need to think more about designing and delivering a positive experience for the customer than about simply selling a product or a service. Starbucks markets a "coffee experience" as customers sit in its attractive shops and escape from the hustle and bustle of the busy world. The famous Barnes & Noble chain of bookstores delivers an experience that includes chairs and tables for sitting and reading, evening lectures and performances, and a great coffee shop. REI, a retailer selling climbing equipment, includes a climbing wall and a simulated rainfall in its stores so that customers can test and experience the performance of its products. Bass PRO, a retailer of fishing equipment, includes a pool of water with fish so that customers can try out the fishing pole. This suggests that marketers should think through the experience that customers have when they obtain a product or service and see how they can provide a simulation of this experience.

What will be the impact of real-time information on the practice of marketing?

I foresee a time when much marketing will be conducted on a real-time battlefield basis, with hard data coming in from the market and being analyzed through marketing decision support programs, with calculated responses simulated and then implemented in the field. This is the model used by the military. A few companies, particularly the major airlines, are operating with a "marketing war gaming room."

Is the trend toward customized products and services still going strong?

The early examples of companies that customized their offerings—computers (Dell), blue jeans (Levi Strauss), bicycles (National), and so on—have shown that customization can work. Customization is practiced even more in business-to-business marketing: The truck manufacturer customizes its trucks for different fleet buyers. More products will come to be customized, but they still will represent only a small percentage of all products.

I want to make it clear that most companies do not need to go into customized marketing. It is usually much more efficient to target and design for segments than to customize for each individual buyer. When a segment is clearly defined, making a standard offering to that segment is often enough.

On the other hand, it is true that the more we know about each individual, the better our chance of winning his business. This is the basis for the popularity of customer relationship marketing (CRM). But the question remains whether the revenue coming from adapting offers to each individual will be sufficient to cover the higher costs of gathering and maintaining current information about each individual. Sometimes it is. For example, Dell is the market leader in computers because Dell can let each customer specify the features of the computer she wants and sell it for a lower price as well. We have seen Internet companies offer tailor-made jeans, loans, mortgages, vitamin pills, and cosmetics, with varying degrees of success. But any company should proceed cautiously in moving to the customization stage.

What are metamarkets? How can companies capitalize on the emergence of metamarkets?

A metamarket facilitates all of the activities involved in obtaining an item for use or consumption. To buy a car, I must choose the car, finance it, and obtain insurance. Thus, Edmunds.com is an online metamarket where I can get information about all cars, search for the best dealer for the car that I want, arrange for a loan, and buy insurance. Another example is theknot.com, an online metamarket for obtaining everything connected with preparing a wedding, including gowns, invitations, gifts, and the like.

Major Challenges

What are the most significant challenges marketers face today?

I would list the following challenges:

1. *Getting better financial measures of the impact of marketing programs.* Marketing has been lax in developing marketing metrics to show what particular expenditures and campaigns have achieved. CEOs are no longer satisfied with measures of how much awareness, knowledge, or preference has been created by marketing programs. They want to know how much sales, profit, and shareholder value has been created. One step in the right direction is at Coca-Cola, where its marketers must estimate the financial impacts of their programs before getting a budget and after spending the money. At least this will produce a financial mindset in Coca-Cola's marketers.

2. *Developing more integrated information about important customers.* Customers come in contact with a company at various touchpoints: by e-mail, by snail mail, by phone, in person, and so on. Yet if these touchpoints are not recorded, the company won't have a 360-degree view of a prospect or customer and therefore is handicapped in developing sound offerings and communications for that customer.

3. *Getting marketing to be the company's designer and driver of market strategy.* Too much marketing today is 1P marketing; that is, marketing deals only with promotion, with other departments heavily determining the product, the price, and the place. I remember a major European airline at which the vice president of marketing confessed that he doesn't set the fare or the product conditions (food, staff, décor) or the flight schedules, but only the advertising and the sales force. How can marketing be effective if the 4Ps are not under unified planning and control?

4. *Facing lower-cost/higher-quality competitors.* As China continues its rapid growth, U.S. firms will face a repeat of the Japanese threat, which consisted of competing with Japanese companies that were able to

offer better products at lower costs. This will force more U.S. companies to shift their production to China, and this will reduce jobs at home.

5. *Coping with the increasing power and demands of mega-distributors.* Mega-retailers such as Wal-Mart, Costco, Target, Office Depot, and others are commanding a larger share of the retail marketplace. Many mega-retailers are carrying store brands that are equal in quality to national brands and lower in price, thus forcing down manufacturers' margins. National-brand companies feel more than ever at the mercy of mega-retailers and are desperately searching for defensive and offensive strategies.

You say that the main economic problem plaguing companies is industry overcapacity. What are the main causes of this problem? How can companies cope with it?

Almost every industry suffers from overcapacity. The world auto industry could probably produce 30 percent more cars without adding another factory. The same can be said for the steel industry and many chemical industries. Customers are scarce, not products. Overcapacity is the result of companies' overoptimism about economic prospects and about their prowess in the marketplace. I have seen many companies plan for a 10 percent increase in sales when the total market is growing by only 3 percent. When this happens, the result is overcapacity and hypercompetition. Hypercompetition can only result in falling prices. The main defenses include (1) building a superior brand, (2) developing more loyal customers who will pay a higher price, (3) and acquiring or merging with other companies to rationalize the supply.

What is the difference between a competitive market and a hypercompetitive market?

Many markets have moved from being *competitive markets* to becoming *hypercompetitive markets*. In a competitive market, a company can usually sustain its market position and competitive advantage. In a hypercompetitive market, there is hardly any sustainable competitive advantage. Rapid technological change and globalization can destroy competitive advantages overnight. The only hope is to practice continuous improvement—some even say continuous breakthroughs. When Jack Welch was CEO of General Electric, he told his people: "Change or die!" Perhaps the only advantage a company can have is an ability to change faster than its competitors.

Companies, of course, should study other companies that have mastered certain processes, whether those be product development, customer retention, or order fulfillment. Benchmarking, however, has two forms: passive, in which one company copies the practices of another; and creative, in which one company copies and improves on a process seen at another company. Creative benchmarking is about bettering the best, not just copying the best. Therefore, benchmarking need not lead to a loss of differentiation.

You write that the customer has become the hunter. What impact does that have on marketing strategies?

Customers now have the power. With the advent of the Internet, they have great amounts of information about brands, prices, product quality, features, and service at their disposal. This is in contrast to the past, when information was largely in the hands of the sellers and the cost of acquiring information was high for the buyers. Today the buyer of a car goes on the Internet, searches for product and price information, and comes armed with the facts to wrest a good price from the seller. The sellers who have the best chance to survive and prosper are those who have found ways, in the words of Jack Welch, to "keep giving the customers more for less . . . while maintaining a profit."

How can a company survive in an environment where the markets are changing faster than the marketing?

Not all companies can survive! This is evidenced by the high rate of bankruptcy and the rapid increase in mergers and acquisitions. When there is too much capacity, mergers help to rationalize that capacity. The companies that will do well will be those that can create and deliver the most value to customers. The task is to assess the trajectory of customer wants accurately.

Deficiencies of Marketing

To what extent are marketers themselves responsible for their own marginalization?

Marketers have been put under intense pressure by management to use promotion to sell what the company makes. Of course, the company's output is partly determined by marketing's statement of the sales forecast. Perhaps marketing can be accused of overoptimism. But there is a deeper issue, namely, that senior management tells marketing what it expects the company to sell, rather than listening to marketing's ideas of what can be sold. Maybe the lesson is that marketing has to be more firm and realistic in stating what can be sold.

What are the major impediments to effective marketing?

In my book *The Ten Deadly Sins of Marketing: Signs and Solutions*, I listed and discussed these major signs of poor marketing and the potential solutions:

TEN DEADLY SINS OF MARKETING

1. The firm is not sufficiently market-focused and customer-driven.
2. The firm doesn't fully understand its target customers.
3. The firm needs to better define its competitors and monitor them.
4. The firm has not managed well its relationships with stakeholders.
5. The firm is not good at finding new opportunities.
6. The firm's marketing plans and planning process are deficient.
7. The firm's product and service policies need tightening.
8. The firm's brand-building and communications efforts are weak.
9. The firm is not well organized to carry on marketing.
10. The firm has not made maximum use of technology.

Can you identify any overall approaches to marketing or business that commonly create a business environment in which the "Ten Deadly Sins of Marketing" are likely to occur?

One major cause of business difficulties is management's tendency to run the business for short-term results. This is especially true of public corporations as opposed to family businesses. Corporations set targets for the year and manipulate everything in order to reach these targets, even if it means sacrificing investments that would build a better long-run future.

A related problem is that companies see themselves as producing products rather than producing customers. Products are easily copied and readily priced down. But customers who really like a firm that has served them well tend to remain with the company and spend more over time.

What are your major disappointments about the state of marketing?

I am appalled by the continuing high rate of new product failure, where something like 80 percent of new consumer packaged goods fail and 30 percent of business-to-business new offerings fail. This is in spite of having great theory about the new product development process and the questions that should be answered at each step before allowing a product under development to move to the next stage.

I also find it embarrassing when direct marketers accept a 1 or 2 percent sales response rate, which means most of the communications were wasted.

I am also unhappy that marketers have not yet developed sufficient tools for measuring marketing ROI or marketing's contribution to shareholder value.

Criticisms of Marketing

Do you think that marketing needs to reinvent itself in the face of antiglobalization protests?

The antiglobalization movement is a mixed bag of causes: labor protection, environmental protection, canceling the debt of developing countries, protests against the harsher side of capitalism, and so on. Some of these causes make sense, and others will hurt the very people they intend to help. I am a strong advocate of free trade and globalization, because I prefer it to regulation, which tends to make a society undynamic and fossilized. As for marketing, there are good and bad practices. Marketing needs to set higher standards of socially responsible conduct. In particular, marketers must pay more attention to the impact of their activities on the environment.

Does marketing only meet needs, or does it create needs?

Marketing does not create needs; needs preexist marketing. Marketing creates wants for specific products and services that might satisfy these needs. Nobody was born wanting a Sony Walkman, but people do have a need for stimulation (music, words). Marketing creates the want for a Sony Walkman as one possible way to satisfy a more basic need. Furthermore, the buyer is not really buying a Sony Walkman; she is buying the expected *service* that the product promises to provide.

Of course, the buyer can buy a brand other than Sony. So each manufacturer struggles to make its brand offering more attractive. This is done through better design, more features, better service, or lower prices, each of which appeals to different buyers. Each competitor needs to clarify its target market and design its product to have superior attractiveness to the people in that target market.

Are customers becoming more cynical about business and marketing?

Consumers have traditionally been cynical toward business, and some of this is deserved. It is not so much being cynical about the products as it is being cynical about the way business exaggerates the benefits of a product, mishandles its employees (downsizing), manipulates politicians through lobbying, and certain other practices. A cynical period is always a great opportunity for other companies to stand out as good citizens because they will earn a disproportional amount of trust and preference.

Some people say that marketing techniques create false images about products and companies. How would you answer that?

Marketers aim to attract attention to their offerings, using the tools of advertising, sales promotion, trade shows, sponsorships, special events, sales presentations, direct mail, and the like. Marketers will exaggerate the positive and eliminate the negative aspects of their offering, much like a lawyer who takes one side of an argument and blows up its positives. At the same time, companies would be wise to avoid creating false images of their products. First, if consumers try the product and are disappointed with its performance, they will tell many others of their disappointment. In this case, the company gained a sale but lost a market. Second, competitors will threaten to sue a company that is trying to gain an advantage by falsifying its product's performance. So while there are plenty of techniques for exaggerating, smart firms will describe their true competitive benefits rather than over-claiming and underperforming.

Skills

What understandings do marketing managers need in order to be successful?

Here is a list of things marketing managers need to understand:

- Marketing managers need the classic skills of market research, new product development, product management, pricing, negotiating, communicating, salesmanship, and channel management.

- Increasingly, marketing managers must have a global orientation so that they can recognize new opportunities.
- Marketing managers must know financial analysis in order to estimate the financial impact of proposed marketing strategies. They should understand breakeven analysis, ROI, EVA, and shareholder value. They should be able to measure the profitability of individual customers, market segments, channels, geographical area, and order sizes.
- Marketing managers need to acquire a good understanding of information technology, devices, and media so that they can use the Internet, database marketing, and telemarketing. In technical fields, the marketing manager must have an engineering or technical background.
- Marketing managers must know the strengths and weaknesses of various communication modalities in order to carry out integrated marketing communication.
- Marketers will need to have a broad understanding of mathematical and statistical methods such as cluster analysis, conjoint analysis, data mining, sales response analysis, marketing mix modeling, and other techniques for interpreting market data and phenomena.
- Marketers need skills in creatively thinking outside the box in order to develop new revenue streams for the company.

In general, is marketing well taught? Do you think that managers put into practice the marketing techniques they learn in business schools? How much of being a successful marketer is about having the right instincts?

Business schools can help develop a person into a good marketer; but instincts, luck, intelligence, and other factors create the great marketers. Marketing programs aim to convey concepts, tools, and leading-company cases to the students. Good marketing is partly a matter of following the rules. Great marketing often happens by breaking the rules.

Careers

What compelling reasons can you give to encourage students to study marketing?

Every student needs to study marketing because it is the force that makes the world go round. Everyone markets, not just companies. You market when you try to find a job, when you seek a loan, when you want to win the apartment. Marketing involves a set of skills for analyzing any market, defining the segments, understanding the needs, developing appropriate and superior offerings, and winning loyalty.

What kinds of people go into marketing?

Marketing tends to appeal to people who like challenges, who like to deal with other people, who like competitive battles, and who like to be innovative and creative.

Marketing continues to attract able people who differ from accounting and financial types in that they are more interested in people than in numbers, and more interested in creating action than reporting it. I think that the quality of people in marketing has gone up. Many more people are coming into brand management or marketing research with MBAs, which should give them a broader picture of business decision making, not just marketing

But there are some deficiencies in the training of marketers that keep them from being more assertive and earning a possible seat on the board. (Note that most companies do not include a professional marketer at the board level). One major deficiency is that marketers are not sufficiently trained in financial language and analysis, in spite of the fact that many have earned MBAs. Therefore, they are at a disadvantage when they are arguing with the CFO for more marketing money or showing more accountability for their past expenditures. Marketers won't get more respect until they are more fluent in the language of finance.

A second deficiency is marketers' limited knowledge of technology. The future lies in technologically supported marketing. Marketing success will depend on software sophistication, handhelds, smart cards, database marketing, sales automation, marketing automation, Internet marketing, e-mail marketing, market modeling, predictive analytics, marketing dashboards, and other high-tech tools.

Could you give a recipe for success for a young professional in marketing?

Marketers must know a lot about marketing research, consumer behavior, advertising, sales promotion, and sales management—the basics of traditional marketing. Today there is a growing need for marketers who have a deep understanding of finance, technology, database marketing, telemarketing, customer relationship marketing, and customer profitability analysis. The ultimate recipe for success is to get great training in marketing and combine it with a creative flair, because in this day and age, companies are desperately seeking new ideas for differentiating their offerings.

How many people in the U.S. are employed as marketers?

There are millions of people in various fields of marketing: retailing, wholesaling, media, product, pricing, advertising, and so on. Within each, there are subspecialists in (say) furniture retailing, grocery retailing, and electronics goods retailing. There are specialists in marketing goods, services, ideas, people, places, organizations, information, and property.

In some large companies, the turnover rate among marketing directors is extraordinarily high—some jobs change every eighteen months. Why the high turnover rate?

There are a number of reasons for the high turnover rate. First, the CEO's job is on the line if he doesn't satisfy the investors' expectations. Consequently, the CEO needs the CMO to deliver the planned revenue performance. But the CEO and the CFO may not give the CMO sufficient funding to achieve the top-line goal. The result is that the CEO fires the CMO and searches for a new CMO who promises to bring a winning new formula to the table.

Conversely, the CMO finds the job frustrating because she is forced to reach for an unreachable sales level with insufficient funds. Furthermore, marketers differ greatly in their theories of how to best market a product. Marketing is far from an exact science, and much of it is an art. Some marketers see promotion as the key to success, others see database marketing as the key to success, and still others see marketing research and deep customer understanding as the key to success. There are enough occasions when marketers adopt the wrong prescriptions for remedying the company's problems to lead to the rapid job turnover among CMOs.

Should a large corporation make sure that at least one marketer sits on its board? Marketers surely have a voice within each product division, but should they have a voice on the corporate board?

CMOs certainly are part of the top management team in individual businesses within the corporation, but more often do not sit on the corporate board. Boards usually are dominated by financial, accounting, and legal types who rarely understand or ask about customers. The reason to include a CMO on the corporate board is to bring the voice of the consumer (VOC) into the highest levels in the company. General Electric recently appointed a CMO, corporate level, in addition to a CMO in each division. They are doing the right thing, but they are the exception.

What makes a successful brand manager?

Successful brand managers typically love brand management and want to run a business rather than specialize in marketing research, advertising, selling, or some other area. Brand management provides a broad picture of a mini-business and develops in its practitioners those skills that could lead to a top management position. My best students were those who combined analytical and people skills. Brand managers must negotiate with many parties and need interpersonal skills and credibility.

Should marketers have more financial training?

Definitely. How else will they make the case for more money and subsequently be accountable for their results?

However, while I want marketers to have strong financial training, I don't want them to overdo it. Financially trained people tend to be more risk-averse and may propose fewer highly innovative initiatives.

Is it true that some people are naturally better at marketing than others?

People vary greatly in such traits as charm, integrity, looks, forcefulness, and creativity. Companies that are seeking salespeople define the traits that they think selling their product requires. Selling insurance requires integrity and good communication skills; selling cosmetics requires a willingness to puff up the benefits. The desirable traits vary greatly among industries.

What career advice would you offer tomorrow's managers?

Fewer managers will spend their whole career within one company. Managers will be more attached to their knowledge specialty than to their current company. There will be an active market for each knowledge specialty, and managers will be on the lookout for opportunities to advance. The key, then, is for tomorrow's managers to study the various knowledge specialties and choose the one that will yield the most long-run market value and personal satisfaction. Companies will need to develop better inducement packages and conditions for attracting or retaining valued knowledge workers.

PART 2

Marketing Strategy

It is increasingly hard to find and keep a competitive advantage, given the rapid copying of products, the radical shortening of product life cycles, the increased information available to customers, and customers' growing defenses against commercial messages. Can companies still achieve competitive advantages?

Granted, it is getting increasingly difficult for companies to create and maintain a competitive advantage. Yet we are constantly surprised by the appearance of new business types, new products, and new services. Whoever thought that coffee could be differentiated? Howard Schultz did this when he started Starbucks. Every society has millions of latent niches waiting to be filled by imaginative entrepreneurs. Consumers and businesses differ greatly in the weights they attach to varying services, product quality, durability, reliability, features and styling, and customization. The creative marketer's task is to spot those niches of demand and fill them in such a way that no one else can quite duplicate the provider's quality and service and relationship.

What marketing strategies work best in today's marketplace?

The key to successful strategic marketing is *focusing, positioning,* and *differentiation.* The company must define its target market carefully. It must communicate a unique benefit positioning. And it must develop valued points of difference in its offerings and services that competitors would find difficult to copy.

In the past, high quality and good service were key factors in winning competitive battles. This was because many companies lacked them. Today, however, quality and service are getting to be commodities. Without high quality and good service, a company loses. With high quality and good service, however, a company doesn't necessarily win. High quality and service are expected. Companies must learn to compete in newer ways, which include an ability to develop and deliver goods faster, an ability to win through better product design, styling, and branding, an ability to augment the offer with more benefits, and an ability to build a long-term, mutually profitable relationship with customers.

Let me mention six types of companies whose strategies I greatly admire:

1. Companies that innovate ways to lower the cost and price of particular goods and services: IKEA, Southwest Airlines, Wal-Mart, Target, Home Depot, Dollar General, and Aldi's.
2. Companies that boost quality to very high levels: Sony, Toyota, Intel, Starbucks.
3. Companies that exhibit a social conscience: Body Shop, Ben & Jerry's, Avon, Kraft.
4. Companies that substantially improve the customers' overall experience: Harley-Davidson, Starbucks.
5. Companies that innovate a new business model: Barnes & Noble, Charles Schwab, FedEx.
6. Companies that discover and dominate niches: Progressive Insurance, Tetra.

What are the major strategies available to market leaders?

Market leaders need to emphasize two strategies. One is to grow the whole market. New buyers are most likely to buy from the leader. The other is to watch for innovations and quickly copy the more effective ones. The market leader doesn't have to innovate (this threatens all of its routines), but it must be a fast copier of any threatening new technology.

What are the major strategies available to challenger firms?

Many market leaders have lost their leadership through failing to modernize their product, bring down their price, or improve their service. Leica used to be the preferred high-quality camera; now it is Nikon. Mercedes used to be the preferred expensive automobile in the United States; now it is BMW. Procter & Gamble's Crest toothpaste was the U.S. leader, and now Colgate has taken the lead. The more that one can make a product and/or its accompanying services different from or better than another, the better the chances of dethroning the leader. In the case of Colgate, its Total brand offered new benefits that were not present in Crest.

Pepsi was catching up with Coca-Cola for a while when it focused on younger people and offered a sweeter taste. But Pepsi's ultimate winning strategy may be to dramatically change the Pepsi image rather than the product.

How can a company determine whether to compete by cultivating operational excellence, product leadership, or customer intimacy, the three disciplines mentioned by Michael Treacy and Fred Wiersema in *The Discipline of Market Leaders*?

Any company is probably already close to being better than its competitors at one of these three disciplines. If this strength is valued by the company's target market, the company should continue to lead from this strength. At the same time, it cannot neglect the other two value disciplines. It must perform at least at an adequate level in the other two disciplines. Unfortunately, it is very difficult and unusual for a company to be superior in all three disciplines.

In business, are there any permanent winners? How long does it take for a marketing strategy to get outdated?

There are no permanent winners. Business is a race without a finishing line. Marketing strategies become outmoded much faster today because markets and technology are changing more rapidly than ever before. Any marketing strategy that works will be copied. There is "strategy convergence," which leads to "strategy decay." An established company can suddenly be devastated by disruptive technologies, new competitor alliances, shifting buyer needs and preferences, or new government regulations. Companies must continually benchmark their competitors to make sure that they are at least delivering the basics. They must start their strategic thinking not only by appraising their current situation but also by imagining plausible future scenarios and how these might affect them.

Do logistics play an important role in competitive strategy?

Logistics may account for 20 percent of the cost of doing business. This far exceeds the cost of advertising and many other marketing costs. Companies that can reduce their logistics costs through using bar codes, automated sorting equipment, and other technologies can gain a tremendous advantage.

The trend in many markets is for convergence between traditionally separate worlds. Consider banking and insurance. The apparently huge profits available from life insurance investments led banks to acquire insurance companies. But it has proved very difficult to realize the convergence potential. Why?

The problem is that banking and insurance products have different characteristics. Checking accounts and credit cards are fast-moving financial services, much like fast-moving consumer goods. In contrast, insurance products are more like durable goods: Purchases are infrequent, the costs can be very high, and the commitment is long-term. Yet banks and insurers try to market these two products under a single brand—which is a bit like Procter & Gamble (P&G) trying to sell both the washing powder and the washing machine.

Many banks have toyed with becoming financial supermarkets. Their thinking is that if they have earned a good corporate reputation, they can cross-sell many other financial products. But the person behind the teller's window is not the person who can sell insurance. The teller might be able to spot people who have a potential interest in insurance and forward this information to the insurance division, but anyone who wants to buy insurance will solicit quotes from a number of competitors. I believe that consumer insurance products will increasingly be purchased over the Internet and based on price comparisons. This doesn't augur well for banks using sales agents to sell insurance.

Supermarkets have toyed with venturing into banking services. Does this make sense?

I applaud mega-retailers who venture into banking services and credit cards. The public does much of its purchasing at these stores, and in-store banking offers a major convenience. Certainly these retailers should have ATMs on their premises, but they should also be prepared to extend credit. For many banking services, in-store banks make more sense than do retail banks themselves. I suspect that Wal-Mart will become a major bank in the future and will figure out how to do this successfully.

Segmentation

What is happening to mass marketing? Does it still work? Is it dead or dying?

The original idea of mass production, mass distribution, and mass advertising was adopted by companies making mass products used by a considerable number of people, such as soap, soup, refrigerators, cars, and so on. Thus P&G made Ivory soap and tried to get everyone to buy it, and Coca-Cola made its cola and tried to get everyone to drink it. But people differ in their tastes, and this affords an opportunity for challengers and niche marketers to go after narrower market segments. In response, the large companies started to differentiate their product offerings for different large segments of the market. P&G offers several different brands of detergent that perform differently. Coca-Cola now offers several different versions of its famous drink.

Thus a company has three possible strategies: Go after everyone with one product (undifferentiated marketing); go after different segments with different products (differentiated marketing); or go after one segment as a specialist (concentrated marketing).

Mass marketing is far from dead. Witness Coca-Cola, Crest toothpaste, McDonald's, and many other mass brands. Yet too many companies put out copycat products. Prices of products in a crowded market will inevitably fall. To avoid so many competitors, each company tries to focus on more narrowly defined markets. The pressure to be more selective has been further pushed by the proliferation of communication channels, so that marketers cannot reach a large audience with one prime-time program. Furthermore, direct marketers are claiming superior results by using mailing lists to identify the best prospects for their offerings instead of using blanket mailings. There are products and circumstances where mass marketing remains effective, especially in countries with fewer channels and competitors. In a growing number of circumstances, however, segment marketing or even one-to-one marketing are proving more effective.

What is the best way to segment a market?

A marketer's goal is to divide the members of a market into different groups according to some shared characteristics. Methods of segmentation have gone through several stages. Initially, researchers turned to *demographic segmentation* because of the ready availability of demographic data. They assumed that different groups of people with different ages, occupations, incomes, and education would exhibit different consumption patterns. Later, researchers moved to *geodemographic segmentation* by adding variables such as where customers lived, and their type of home.

Having discovered that people within these demographic segments do not necessarily exhibit the same consumption patterns led researchers to adopt *behavioral segmentation* by classifying people according to their readiness to buy, motivation, and attitude. One form was *benefit segmentation,* which clustered customers according to the main benefit they sought from the product. Another form was *psychographic segmentation,* which clustered people based on their lifestyle characteristics.

More recently, researchers have pursued *loyalty segmentation* by paying more attention to customers who could be retained longer and more profitably than other customers.

When all is said and done, segmentation analysis is a search for insight into customers and customer types, and it can provide a rich reward for marketers who are the first to identify new variables for classifying customers.

How can a company proceed to find niches in the market?

Niches exist in every market. One has to study what the different buyers in a market want in the way of product attributes, prices, channels, shipment times, and other features. You will begin to find that buyers fall into distinct groups, with each group valuing a certain product/service/relationship configuration. Any group can be a niche that some company decides to specialize in serving.

For example, an architectural firm can offer to design any type of edifice or choose to specialize in a particular type, such as nursing homes, hospitals, prisons, or college dormitories. After choosing nursing homes, the firm can further specialize by offering design services for high-priced nursing homes instead of low-priced nursing homes. The architectural firm can further choose to work only within the state of Florida. Thus this firm has chosen the niche of designing high-priced nursing homes in Florida. Presumably its research showed that this niche was sufficiently large and profitable.

How is the Internet used for reaching market segments?

The Internet facilitates market segmentation. I am quite impressed with web sites that are dedicated to a specific segment, such as new mothers with babies, senior citizens,

Hispanics, and other groups. I expect to see scores of web sites that serve specific affinity groups by providing information, shopping, and interaction opportunities.

Today's Web merchants are building a "data warehouse" with the names of customers and prospects and much information about each. They are "data mining" their data warehouse and discovering new segments and niches. Then they e-mail their offerings to their best prospects. This is classic market segmentation.

Targeting

Should a company spend more time attracting new customers or retaining old ones?

Marketers historically have focused on the problem of attracting new customers. Salespeople were rewarded more for finding a new customer than for paying a lot of attention to existing customers. Now companies are paying more attention to the art of keeping customers. They have heard that it might cost five times as much to attract a new customer as to retain an existing customer. We are moving from "producing products" to "producing loyal customers," from a transaction orientation to a relationship orientation. In the past we relied on the customer service department to handle this, but relationship marketing involves much more than running a good customer service department. It involves skills in increasing "customer share" through cross-selling and upselling.

How much "narrowcasting" do you advocate?

Marketers must increasingly turn from "broadcasting" to "narrowcasting" their messages. People are not interested in most of the messages that reach them through TV or radio. They "zap" TV commercials and skip the ads in newspapers unless an ad is in an area of interest to them. The first rule of marketing communication is to define the target customers and their media habits. Messages must be put into focused media. A fishing pole should be advertised in a fishing magazine, and a new motorcycle should be advertised in a motorcycle magazine.

Should a company keep pursuing worthwhile prospects until it succeeds, or should it establish a cutoff point?

Salespeople face this question all the time. A salesperson may have called on a purchasing agent five times, taking the person to lunch and dinner and showing other courtesies. But there still is no sale! Should the salesperson continue to court this account, or should he give up? Most companies establish a cutoff point to keep their salespeople from overinvesting time and expense in no-response prospects.

I recommend establishing cutoff points. I remember a university fundraiser who wined and dined a certain wealthy widow for years. She kept implying that she would put money for the university in her will. In the meantime, she was also being pursued by several other universities. It was clear that she was enjoying all the attention. My advice is that this fundraiser should ask for a formal commitment now or stop courting her.

Is it better to target easy-to-sell-to prospects who don't spend much or hard-to-sell-to prospects who, if attracted, will spend a great deal?

This requires estimating the expected value of a prospect. Suppose an easy-to-sell prospect is likely to spend $100 with an 80 percent probability. The expected value is $80. Suppose a hard-to-sell prospect is likely to spend $1,000 with a 30 percent probability. Here the expected value is $300. Using this criterion, the marketer should pursue the hard-to-sell prospect. This has to be further qualified. Suppose the salesperson can pursue five easy-to-sell prospects in the time it takes to pursue one hard-to-sell prospect. Then the expected value of pursuing five easy-to-sell prospects is $400 (5 × $80) for the same time involved in pursuing one hard-to-sell prospect with an expected value of $300.

I have noticed that universities that have limited solicitation resources tend to pursue a few wealthy individuals rather than move into a mass marketing effort to attract small amounts from many individuals. The thinking is that getting one wealthy person to donate $1 million is worth much more than getting 10,000 alumni to donate $1,000 each. In practice, however, most universities carry on both activities.

Positioning

Some people believe that positioning is the key step in marketing. Do you agree?

Positioning is only one step in effective marketing. Effective marketing begins with research into the local marketplace to discover segments that might be dissatisfied with the current offerings. The company then chooses target segments to which it can provide a superior offering. Positioning is the next step, whereby the company communicates what it offers to the target market segments. Note that the company cannot position without first doing segmentation and targeting.

For example, the Volvo automobile company discovered that there was a sufficient size segment of car buyers who placed a very high value on car safety, but no car company offered superior car safety. Volvo adopted "safest car" as its positioning.

But positioning by making this claim is not enough. Volvo had to actually make the safest car, or else competitors and customers would find out that the claim was not true. Not only did Volvo have to make the safest cars, but it had to design the cars' looks and "feel" to signal their superior safety. It also had to convey the safety theme repeatedly in all its advertising and promotion.

What is your opinion about big company mergers? Al Ries writes about losing focus, and suggests that companies selling different kinds of products shouldn't merge. What's your opinion on this?

I am less concerned than Al Ries about a company selling different products. P&G sells hundreds of products and does well. I am more concerned with whether the merger makes good sense. Does it eliminate duplicate costs? Does it combine complementary activities and skills? Does the merger benefit from any synergies? I view less favorably conglomerate mergers that simply make a company bigger but not better.

Differentiation

What are the key ways today in which a company can gain a marketing edge?

Managers today are attending the same seminars, learning about the value of benchmarking, outsourcing, and exceeding competitors' offers. But the playing field is never static because each competitor starts with a different set of resources, competencies, and opportunities. Alert companies will discover and quickly implement competitive advantages. Market shares will shift with the inventiveness of the different players.

Consider the automobile industry. Henry Ford made cost his firm's competitive advantage, then GM made variety and styling its competitive advantage, then the Europeans and the Japanese made quality their competitive advantage. Today Japan is working on developing sensuous automobiles . . . owners will take pleasure from just opening and closing the door or turning on the radio. American companies and certain automobile dealers are rediscovering the power of good service. No competitive platform works forever or for all buyers.

Companies must learn to compete in newer ways, which include an ability to develop and deliver goods faster, to win through better product design and styling, to augment the offer with more benefits, and to build a long-term, mutually profitable relationship with customers. Companies need to consider new features, superior design, better aesthetics, customization, better and more services, and more customer intimacy.

What should be the strategy for a company in a commodity line of business?

I believe that many commodities (e.g., steel, plastics, and chemicals) will be increasingly traded on *electronic markets*. Vertical hubs such as plastics.com, steel.com, and chemdex .com already exist, and their business volume is growing. The implication is that price will be key to the success of commodity companies. Only the most efficient companies (those that can charge a lower price and still earn a satisfactory margin) will be the winners.

Yet buying a commodity is not simple. The buyer wants the assurance of consistent quality, reliable delivery, volume discounts, and other features that allow commodity companies to compete on the basis of offering the "lowest total cost of ownership or use."

We pay very different prices for a commodity such as coffee. Coffee purchased in a store and made at home costs about 25 cents a cup. A cup of coffee in an ordinary restaurant costs about $1.00. A cup of coffee in Starbucks can cost from $2.00 to $4.00. All this illustrates the danger of thinking that a commodity cannot be differentiated.

Can a commodity such as electricity be differentiated? What segments and niches are there in the energy market?

In South Africa, I met an energy executive who has branded different electrical energy services. There is a different price depending on whether the electricity is generated by coal, nuclear power, water power, or windmills. The company has developed different pricing programs for different use occasions. For example, customers who can postpone using their electrical service until the middle of the night get a much lower price.

Innovation

What is the role of innovation in marketing?

As Peter Drucker said, "A business has two—and only two—basic functions: marketing and innovation. Marketing and innovation produce results: all the rest are costs." This suggests that a winning formula (used by Sony, 3M, and Pfizer) is to have Great Innovation + Great Marketing. Innovation is not only about creating new and better products but also about developing better systems and new business concepts. Companies such as IKEA, Southwest Airlines, Virgin, Home Depot, and Barnes & Noble invented new ways to run old industries and have been profit leaders. Marketers play a critical role in suggesting innovations, estimating their potential, and refining their features and launch plans.

Why is innovation important?

Innovation is not universally regarded as important or desirable. There are people who would prefer that innovation stop. They don't like change. On the other hand, many Americans love change. It comes out of the belief that innovation means progress. Americans believe that they can eventually create a heaven on earth where medical remedies exist for every disease, every experience will be available through virtual reality, there are great-tasting foods that are also nutritious, and political differences can be settled without resorting to violence.

Yet innovation calls for creativity, which is sorely lacking. What can marketers do to address the lack of creativity?

Companies can become more creative in three ways. The first is to hire more people with a creative bent, whose minds are more free-wheeling, more curious, more questioning. The second is to employ creativity tools and processes in the course of solving company problems. Such tools include brainstorming, synectics, modification analysis, forced relations, and morphological analysis. The third is to occasionally hire the services of a creative agency, one that offers to help generate big new ideas for a company.

Which innovations do you consider to be landmarks in the history of marketing?

Here are some pioneering developments that have changed our lives and lifestyles:

- Retail innovations such as the department store, the supermarket, the hypermarket, "category killer" stores, convenience stores, mega-retailers, shopping malls, and fast-food restaurants
- Market logistics innovations such as FedEx, container shipments, and cross-docking
- Quality innovations such as zero defects, six-sigma quality, and total quality management teams
- New sales channels such as direct mail, telemarketing, fax marketing, and online marketing
- Physical inventions such as the telephone, the radio, TV, computers, cellphones, and the Internet
- Financial innovations such as the credit card, installment buying, and money-back guarantees of satisfaction

How can we push innovation?

In most companies, there are good ideas floating around, but there is no net to catch them. I advise companies to establish an *idea management system* headed by a senior officer who works with a multidiscipline committee. The idea management committee has a pool of money to use to investigate promising ideas. Every employee and company partner (e.g., distributors, dealers, and suppliers) should know the e-mail address of the senior officer to propose market or cost improvement ideas, and to be rewarded for those ideas that lead to increased profits. Companies such as Toyota and Whirlpool treat all of their employees as potential innovators. Toyota claims that it receives about thirty-five improvement suggestions per employee per year. This comes from the Japanese ethic called *kaizen*, "everybody improving everything all the time." Companies can train their personnel in brainstorming and other creativity methods, as well as provide suggestion boxes and reward the best idea creators with honors and/or cash.

Are there any general rules allowing us to minimize the risk that a new product will not be accepted by the market?

Marketers can use fairly reliable techniques to test ordinary new product ideas. However, the more radical the idea, the more difficult it is to reliably forecast demand. When VCRs were introduced, people were confused about what they were. Even if consumers grasped the idea, they couldn't tell whether they would buy the product. How would it make a difference in their lives? Is it priced reasonably in relation to its alleged benefits?

A radically new product calls for a process of *testing and learning* from the moment it is conceived and certainly from the moment it is introduced into the marketplace. Initial sales (or refusals) present an opportunity to learn and to fix the offering or the communications or the pricing.

What do you think is a better marketing investment for a company, innovation or improvement?

If you ask Japanese companies, they would prefer constant improvement to product innovation (with the exception of

Sony and a few others). This made sense because when the Japanese came into the global market, they noticed poor quality U.S. products (automobiles and appliances, for example), so they could win by simply making the products better. Yet products in some categories reach a point of near perfection. How can you make a detergent better? At that point, the company has to shift its bet to innovating something new. This calls for thinking more fundamentally and out of the box. Yet innovation involves greater cost and risk, and this keeps a lot of companies from tackling innovation as a route to success.

PART 3

Marketing Tools (the 4Ps)

Who came up with the famous 4Ps?

Professor Jerry McCarthy introduced the scheme in his first edition of *Marketing* (circa 1960). He took his Ph.D. at Northwestern University and studied under Professor Richard Clewett, who used the framework product, price, distribution, and promotion. Jerry changed "distribution" to "place" and could then talk about the 4Ps. My books are credited with popularizing the 4Ps, but my main contribution was to say that the 4Ps are tactical and must be preceded by strategic decisions on STP, namely segmentation, targeting, and positioning.

Are the 4Ps still a useful framework for marketing decision making?

The 4Ps still provide a useful framework for marketing planning. However, they represent the seller's thinking more than the buyer's thinking. The 4Ps can be converted to the 4Cs as follows:

Product becomes customer value.

Price becomes customer costs.

Place becomes customer convenience.

Promotion becomes customer communication.

The 4Cs remind us that customers want value, low total costs, high convenience, and communication, not promotion.

Professor Jagdish Sheth has suggested an alternative scheme called the 4As. For customers to buy, there must be awareness, acceptability, affordability, and accessibility.

Others have proposed adding other Ps to the 4Ps: packaging, personal selling, passion, and so on. Packaging is actually subsumed under product or promotion, and personal selling and passion are subsumed under promotion.

Three additional Ps have been proposed for guiding service marketing. Personnel is one, in that each service provider will make a certain impression. Process is a second one, in that service can be provided in many different ways: For example, food from a restaurant can be available through table service, buffet, and home delivery. Physical evidence suggests that service marketers seek to give their offerings a tangible character by using certificates, tickets, logos, and so forth.

I have made a case for including politics and public opinion (which I have called megamarketing tools), since much of marketing depends upon a receptive government and a receptive public. If governments discriminate against multinationals, for example, multinationals will be less effective. Therefore, multinationals must persuasively market their benefits and potential contributions to the economy of the host country, using politics and public opinion.

Can you please say something regarding "the need for a new marketing mix?"

The original marketing mix was not 4Ps but about fourteen. Neil Borden many years ago used a large list of marketing tools. We can always add to the list. So the question isn't "what tools constitute the marketing mix?" but rather, "what tools are becoming more important in the marketing mix." For example, I feel that advertising is overdone and public relations is underdone. This is seconded in Al Ries's new book, *The Fall of Advertising and the Rise of PR*. And direct-marketing tools are also rising in importance in the marketing mix.

What new tools are available to marketers?

Marketers rely on information. There are new software tools for managing information better. Many salespeople today use sales automation software to help them answer questions in the customers' offices and close the sale.

New software promises to help rationalize other marketing decisions. For example, the airlines use yield-pricing software to change the prices of airline fares on a daily basis depending on how occupied a specific flight is before the time of flight.

Some companies are putting their main marketing processes on the computer so that they are available to every product and brand manager. The manager turns on the computer and follows the steps outlined in the process, whether it is to test a concept, to market test a new product, or to choose a new advertising agency. It is like building a marketing consultant into the computer.

A number of software companies are developing software to manage different marketing processes, such as *Emmperative, E. piphany,* and *Unica,* among others.

Who will benefit most from the use of the Internet? Businesses or customers?

Customers will benefit the most. Prices will become more transparent. Customers will be able to order their specific version of a product, as in the case of buying a Dell computer over the Internet. Customers will be less assaulted by intrusive large-page ads. As for businesses, those that align with the new technologies will benefit greatly (i.e., Yahoo!, Amazon, and so on), and others will suffer as e-commerce threatens them with obsolescence.

What do you think about the future of marketing models?

Larger companies are gaining advantages in using certain marketing models and statistical tools. Conjoint analysis permits them to figure out the best set of features to build into a market offering. There are sales force models for determining the optimal size for the sales force and the optimal territorial coverage. Companies are using sophisticated data-mining techniques to discover hidden patterns in customer databases. My coauthored book *Marketing Models* outlines many of these models.

Product

Brands and Branding

What are the reasons for the branding hype during the last decade?

Brands provide the major defense against price competition. Strong brands create more trust and comfort and an image of better quality than less well known brands. People are willing to pay a price premium for the stronger brands. But it should be understood that a brand is not strong simply because it spends more advertising money. The ultimate strength of a brand is based on its performance, not its promotion. We say that a brand is initially built by publicity and advertising and ultimately maintained by its performance.

Companies are realizing that brands are their only hope of gaining attention and respect in the increasingly competitive marketplace. A brand is a promise of value. It becomes the organizing concept for all the company's activities that surround the brand. Thus, if Motorola claims that its quality is six sigma (only three defects per million), then every activity must be orchestrated to deliver on this promise. Once marketers began to see each brand as standing for being the best in some area of customer preference, then they recognized the need to go beyond the 4Ps of product, price, place, and promotion. The brand became the strategy lever and activity organizer for the company's efforts in the marketplace. A successful brand shifts the demand curve to the left, allowing the company to either sell more for the same price or charge a higher price and sell the same quantity.

Do you think that honing a strong brand image is enough to sell a product?

Normally not. Those who favor image believe that a strong brand image can create preference in the absence of other differences. How can you explain Marlboro's success except through the cowboy image? Others think that images are converging and losing their power to command high brand premiums. The key need is to develop a distinctive offering, not simply a distinctive image. The offering can be distinctive in features, styling, services, service support, guarantees, and a host of other factors that will make one value proposition superior to another in the eyes of the beholder. I am in favor of building a superior value proposition, not just massaging an image.

What kind of brands do you expect to be the successful brands of tomorrow?

I will distinguish between mass-market brands and niche brands. Mass-market brands need to deliver values that are on the minds of most consumers. If consumers are becoming more cost-conscious, then winning brands will be those that feature good value for the money. Examples would be private-label brands, low-cost airline brands, low-cost furniture brands (IKEA), and so on. If consumers start preferring companies that are more environmentally and socially responsible, then brands that reflect social values will be the winners.

Niche brands succeed more through recognizing a narrow and neglected need in sections of the population and developing an offering that satisfies this need better than any mass product can do. I think the future belongs to niche brands because of growing market fragmentation and growing customer insistence.

What do you mean by "moving from brands to brand asset management?" Why is this important?

Brands are marketing assets with real market value. Interbrand and other companies provide estimates of the market value of different leading global brands. A company that wanted to buy the brand name Coca-Cola would have to pay over $70 billion, many times more than Coca-Cola's book value. This means that a high percentage of Coca-Cola's worth is in intangibles.

Every successful brand becomes a platform for further

extensions. Consider Disney: The name now covers films, videotapes, theme parks, hotels, cruise ships, toys, and retail stores. So it is not surprising that companies with strong brands must manage them carefully, keeping them fresh and finding proper ways to extend the brand name into new domains. You can't leave brand management to the brand manager alone, partly because of brand manager turnover, and partly because a brand manager may be tempted to cut brand maintenance costs to achieve a higher short-run profit.

How do you build a brand?

This is a question that requires reading a whole book for the answer. Scores of books have been written on how to build a brand. Each author offers a framework and a set of concepts based on his or her marketing knowledge and experience. I happen to like the books by David Aaker, Jean Noel Kapferer, and Scott M. Davis, although many of the other books are also very informative.

Do you think that global brands can be developed by companies in smaller countries?

A small country such as Switzerland (population: nine million) has dozens of highly visible brand names . . . Nestlé, Swatch, Rolex, ABB, Hoffman LaRoche, Bauer, and so on. The same goes for Sweden (population: five million) . . . Volvo, Saab, Electrolux, Ericsson, Sandvik. Many large countries, such as Russia, India, China, and Brazil, have, ironically, few global brands that we can name. Country size is not that important.

How can a local brand become a global brand?

A local brand will remain local unless it is different from and better than products in the same category found in other markets. The local brand needs to move through a succession of countries and/or regions on its way to becoming global. The Mexican beer Corona made a successful entry into the United States by first entering U.S. cities with strong Mexican populations. Afterwards it expanded slowly into northern U.S. cities. Today it is the number one imported beer in the United States. It still is not a player in the European market. A local brand may have to strategize for ten to twenty years before achieving global prominence.

Do you think that global companies that localize their offerings and communications do better than those that standardize their offerings and communications?

Yes, generall speaking. McDonalds lost its number-one position in the Philippines to Jollibees, a local fast-food chain that adapted its offerings better to Philippine tastes. The same thing happened in Greece when Goodies, a local fast-food chain, surpassed McDonalds.

Global companies make the common mistake of using standardized offerings and communications everywhere. Although this is cheaper to do, it is more expensive in the long run. A company needs to adapt its offerings, value proposition, messages, media, and channels to each country.

Many local company brands have been acquired by multinationals. Is this the best way to enter a foreign market?

A multinational that wishes to enter a country can bring in its own brand, buy an existing local brand, or invent a new brand for that country. Bringing in its own brand makes sense if its brand is highly regarded and is seen as delivering more quality or value than the local brands. Buying a local brand makes sense if it has widespread local preference and growth potential, and would be more popular than the foreign brand. Inventing a new brand would be expensive but could make sense if neither the foreign brand nor the local brand really meets the needs of the local market.

Should a multinational that uses several brand names for the same product in different countries fold these local names into one brand name?

Some large multinationals eventually replace some of their local brand names with global brand names. The Mars company has been the most aggressive in this regard. In England, its candy bar called Marathon was changed to Snickers, the U.S. name, and its Treets was changed to M&Ms, again the U.S. name. A company can save a lot of advertising and packaging money by building a global brand, or at least a Eurobrand. This also means that travelers going to different countries can easily recognize the brand. At the same time, the company is giving up a local name in which it built a lot of local equity. Procter & Gamble (P&G), for example, sells the same shampoo under three names: Pert in the United States, Vidal Sasson in France, and Rejoy in Japan. Making Pert the global name would require a heavy investment to educate users of the other brand names about the name change and induce them to accept it. This is aside from the question of whether the global name is pronounceable and does not have any negative associations in other languages.

A brand's reputation is difficult to obtain and easy to lose. How does a brand keep its leadership?

Brands are subject to a life cycle. When certain brands first appear, such as McDonald's or Levi's jeans or Nike shoes or Swatch watches, they may be lucky and create excitement and enter into a strong growth phase. After a while, these brands begin to lose some of their luster as people start taking them for granted and as some customers migrate to new competitive offerings or new interests. This is a crisis time for the brand. The brand now needs rejuvenation, and the task of the brand asset management is to inject new benefits and meanings into the brand.

Do you think private brands are a growing threat to national and global brands? What can national brands do about this?

Private brands are the greatest threat facing national and global brands. I foresee a time when supermarket chains will carry 50 percent private brands. Private brands started out years ago as cheaper and lower-quality offerings to satisfy lower-income consumers. Then Loblaws, a supermarket chain in Canada, introduced its President's Choice brand of soft drinks, cookies, and other items, made at a quality level as good as or even better than the national brands. Still later, it occurred to supermarkets that they might run two or three private brands: good, better, and best. Today's customers are increasingly relying on these brands, which can save them 10 to 50 percent of the cost. For example, the large Walgreen's drugstore chain in the United States puts out a Walgreen's brand in most categories that is often priced at half the cost of the national brand. A company such as Wal-Mart is beginning to recognize that its consumers are so loyal to the store that Wal-Mart might as well put out Wal-Mart's brands of soft drinks, detergents, diapers, and other mass products.

National brands have the following strategy options for fighting store brands:

- Reduce the price of the national brand
- Innovate new features

- Keep improving quality
- Strengthen brand image
- Show the retailer that he makes more money giving shelf space to the national brand

If you could market any brand that has existed during your lifetime, what would it be?

Microsoft. It has a virtual monopoly, and it has made Bill Gates the richest man in the world. Besides, the business is technical and challenging.

What makes a great brand?

There are five dimensions to a strong brand. First, a brand should bring to mind certain attributes, such as the product's features, style, and so on. Second, the brand should strongly suggest one or more key benefits. For example, Volvo connotes safety and Apple connotes user-friendliness. Third, we should be able to visualize the brand's characteristics, as if the brand were a person: Apple would be in his twenties and IBM in his sixties. Fourth, the brand should suggest something about the company's values: Is the company innovative, customer responsive, or socially conscious? Finally, a strong brand suggests a picture of the brand's users—are they young and enthusiastic or older and more established? Brand marketers must develop all five factors to make a brand robust.

Great brands conjure up images, expectations, and promises of performance. They have a personality: Consider the many associations that come to mind when we mention McDonald's, Apple Computer, Club Med, Swatch watches, and Harley-Davidson.

What should you never do with a brand?

Never stop improving the brand. The competitors will always be adding new features and services to make inroads on your brand. Your company must be the leader in enhancing the brand and introducing the brand to new users, and even entering the brand into new categories. As Andy Grove said, "Only the paranoid survive."

Unfortunately, many brands are only supported with reminder communications and stale ads. This is largely a waste of money until you have new points to make about your brand.

Many brands are trying to find their place in customers' hearts. What kinds of brands will succeed?

A person's attitude toward a brand may range from dislike to indifference to slight preference to strong preference to devotion. Everyone has preferred brands, but few brands create devoted fans. Those with devoted fans include Harley-Davidson, Porsche, Apple Computer, Bang & Olufsen, and a few others. Certain vehicles, heavy appliances, software, and music groups command loyal audiences. Most ordinary brands, however, are lucky if they can gain slight or strong preference. Those that succeed make a better and distinctive promise that they consistently deliver.

Do you agree that the Internet is likely to weaken branded goods because people will be purchasing on price alone?

Brands will remain important in Internet purchasing. Many buyers will still buy a Dell computer even when cheaper computers are available on the Internet. What a specific Internet vendor won't be able to do is to sell a specific product, say a Palm Pilot V, for a much higher price than other Internet vendors are charging. I clicked on a web page, my simon.com, to compare the prices charged for a Palm Pilot V by different Internet vendors: The prices ranged from a high of $449 to a low of $389. The bottom line is that we will still have favorite brands, but the Internet will make it possible to buy them at the lowest available price.

Will the Internet help companies deepen their brand image?

Companies have seen an opportunity to use their web sites as an additional force for branding the company as a whole or its individual products. The visitor to a web site forms an impression of the company or its brand from the look and feel of the web site. Is the site simple to download and easy to use, and does it provide full and clear information? Companies have set up web sites for individual brands. One of the best sites is www.tide.com, for the P&G detergent. The site explains how detergents work and why Tide offers the best cleaning power and value.

Service

So much has been written about service as a key differentiator, but in many places it seems to get worse. Why?

Companies today are developing better customer sensitivity, but they're also cutting costs. These two forces operate in opposite directions. In talking to the customers of a large bank that has increased its service orientation, its customers told me that they think its service is worse! The explanation? At the same time that the bank trained its people to be more customer-oriented, it eliminated some tellers, so the lines are longer. When you finally reach the teller, the teller is friendly, but there aren't enough tellers. That explains this paradox of service getting better and worse at the same time.

In the midst of this bind, companies must start distinguishing among their customer groups. Not all customers make money for the company. Companies need to define who are their important customers and make sure that they are served even better than before.

In markets today there are very few pure products, and everything is a combination of product and services. What is the role of the service component?

Actually, the service component of an offering is likely to make a bigger difference than the product component, because so many products are similar. Services are more difficult to copy and execute well by competitors. A smart marketer can create a "service surround" to the product, which is unique and difficult to imitate. Yet many companies are product-fixated and, unfortunately, regard service as an afterthought in the design of their offering. They worry too much about the cost of smart service and pay too little attention to its impact.

Are the Internet and e-commerce going to reduce the need for personal service?

Customers vary greatly in their appetite for personal service. Many customers simply want to transact business in the easiest way with a minimum of chit-chat. Other customers want hand-holding. I find it interesting that some of the most admired companies do all, or most, of their business by phone or Internet. Consider USAA insurance or L. L. Bean or Dell or Schwab, which conduct most of their business over a phone or on the Internet. And customers will say that their service is extraordinary.

Price

What price premium can a superior brand charge?

Before hypercompetition, globalization, and the Internet set in, superior brands could charge anywhere from 20 to 50 percent more than the average brand. Today, a superior brand is lucky if it can charge 10 to 20 percent more.

What is the impact of the Internet on pricing?

On one of the Internet sites, priceline.com, buyers propose what they would pay for a specific airline trip or hotel, leaving it up to the sellers to decide whether they are willing to sell at that price. This may eventually extend to buying cars, collectibles, and other products. My strong feeling is that the Internet will drive down prices and margins for many goods. Prices are much more transparent on the Internet. One can go to a shopping bot such as buy.com or compare.com and see what various Internet e-tailers are charging for a specific item. Buyers will find great price variation for specific consumer electronics items, specific books, and so on. If they regard the sellers as offering comparable service, they will buy from the lowest-price e-tailer.

It is said that consumers are becoming very price-sensitive, and therefore marketers can do little but lower the price. Do you agree?

I don't think consumers are becoming more price-sensitive so much as value-sensitive. When they buy on price, it is because they see little difference between the higher- and lower-priced products. Those companies that can create and communicate more value through features, style, value-adds, and other differentiators will be able to command a higher price. This involves careful targeting of the customer segment and understanding its total needs as they relate to the product.

Buyers can actually be divided into three groups:

- The strictly price-conscious buyer
- The buyer who will pay a little more for better quality or service, but only up to a limit
- The buyer who wants the very best quality and service

Accordingly, the firm should target one of these groups and create the product/service offering that appeals to that target group.

What can manufacturers do when they face lower-price competitors?

Companies are justifiably worried about competition coming from lower-price countries and companies. I know of a fine European manufacturer of leaded crystal for chandeliers that is now facing a competitor from Egypt that can offer crystal at 50 percent less. Either the European manufacturer will lobby for high tariffs to protect the company against lower-cost imports or it will have to reduce its costs and margins drastically. In the latter case, this could require reengineering, downsizing, increased automation, decreased tax burdens, and so on. Or the company needs to add new benefits missing from its competitors' offerings. Or the company might acquire the low-price competitor.

Do you have any thoughts for the marketer who is trying to devise a strategy to compete with low-cost Chinese companies?

The first tendency of companies that are hurt by lower prices coming out of China is to lobby for protection. Protection can take two forms: (1) raising tariffs on cheaper foreign imports or (2) preventing local companies from moving overseas in search of lower costs.

But these efforts are short-lived and are likely to be counterproductive. The real answer lies in each company searching for better ways to offer superior value to specific target groups of customers. It will not be possible to hold on to customers who consider only price when your costs are higher. But there are always customers who want added value in terms of product quality, various services, delivery reliability, customization, consulting help, or other benefits. Each business unit has to think through how to build a superior brand for those target customers who want to receive superior value for their money.

How prevalent are price wars?

The art of marketing is the art of branding. If you are not a brand with a difference, you will face price competition and price wars. And the only winners will be the firms with the lowest costs and prices.

We don't see many price wars in the United States. Sometimes they break out in commodities, such as gasoline, airfares, certain chemicals, and steel. Minor brands of gas can charge two cents less, but if they charge four cents less, major brands will retaliate. But there are few price wars in many markets, such as detergents, toothpaste, and shampoos.

There is the normal sales promotion competition, but no price warfare.

In many countries, sales are won by offering bribes. How should a marketer think and act in regard to corruption?

Corruption distorts the normal process of competition, where the buyer is assumed to choose among suppliers based on which one offers the most value for the money. For example, a company that needs delivery trucks ought to buy the brand whose trucks best fit the company's purposes for the best price. If the buyer chooses poorer trucks because she receives a bribe, the buyer's company will suffer as a result of poorer truck performance. Corruption, therefore, is antithetical to the whole marketing philosophy of maximizing market satisfaction and performance. That being said, where corruption exists, a competitor must acknowledge it and try to expose it rather than practice it.

Place (Distribution)

Do companies do a sufficient job of thinking through distribution?

All companies should painstakingly research the different channel alternatives available to distribute their products. The greater the number of distribution channels, the greater the company's reach into the market. Still, two problems arise.

The first one is market control. As we sell through more channels, control becomes more difficult. Therefore, it is essential that the company develop control processes to monitor key indicators of performance in the different distribution channels.

The second problem is channel conflict. For example, if a company that sells through dealers adds a direct-selling e-commerce channel, the dealers will resent this. They won't want to compete with the supplier's e-commerce selling channel and may withdraw their distribution. This problem has to be dealt with by brick-and-click companies.

What should be done with a manufacturer who doesn't understand and accommodate to satisfy the trade?

Distributors and retailers are becoming more powerful, and they control the path to the customer. Manufacturers must build win-win relationships with important trade partners. In the old days, strong manufacturers paid as little as possible to the trade because the trade had to carry their products. Now the trade often has the power to demand better terms from manufacturers or to refuse to carry the manufacturer's products. Most enlightened manufacturers are seeking partnerships with major trade groups, instead of adversarial relationships. They are going further and tailoring a special trade relationship with each major distributor.

How many channels of distribution should a company use?

The number of channels for buying any product are multiplying. One can buy a product by going to the store or by purchasing it by mail, telephone, kiosk, or the Internet. A company that uses only one marketing channel for product distribution will face competition from all the other channels. Prices may also be quite different depending on the channel. Therefore, a company must carefully choose which channel(s) to use to establish its market presence. The more channels a company uses, the more the managerial resources needed and the greater the chance for channel conflict and confusion. Yet it is critical for a company to develop brand consistency and deliver on its brand promise wherever its products are sold.

How can a company sell to some customers directly without losing the support of the middleman channel?

The company has three choices:

1. Draw a line between the large customers that it handles directly and the smaller customers that resellers will handle.
2. Develop a product that will be sold directly to customers that differs from what the reseller sells. (In the case of personal computers, the reseller might sell low-powered computers and the company might sell high-powered computers directly.)
3. Decide to drop the middleman and only sell direct.

One of the main concerns for companies selling through traditional channels is the competition coming from purely online marketers. What should traditional marketers do?

Bricks-and-mortar companies initially worried that pure click competitors would take away their business. The opposite happened: The smart bricks-and-mortar companies added brick-and-click, and they were much better known by the public and had more financial resources than the pure click companies. Thus the Barnes & Noble bookstore chain added a web site, giving people the choice of coming into the store or ordering online from a much larger book selection. The problem was different for a company like Compaq, which was losing computer sales to direct marketer Dell. If Compaq sold direct, it would alienate its retail partners. However, Compaq found a way to sell online as well as through retailers: It gave a commission to those retailers in the service area of any customer who purchases a Compaq online. In general, companies have to figure out different solutions to harmonizing selling through retailers and selling online.

Promotion

TV advertising seems to be losing its effectiveness. What are alternative ways to get attention?

The average American is exposed to several hundred ad messages a day and is trying to tune out. TV advertising is losing its effectiveness because of growing advertising clutter, the increasing number of channels, the availability of zapping mechanisms, and reduced watching of television by certain groups. The result is that marketers must consider other methods of getting consumer attention. Here are a number of possibilities:

- *Sponsorships.* Companies have put their names on stadiums, on whole teams, and on individual athletes in order to gain exposure.
- *Mentions on talk shows.* During his evening show, David Letterman sent a camera crew out to buy Snickers candy bars and ended up talking about it on three subsequent shows, including when Mars sent a whole van of Snickers to feed the audience.

- *Product placement.* In *Die Another Day,* James Bond drove an Aston Martin, used a Sony cell phone, and prominently featured an Omega wristwatch. Products are also mentioned in novels—in fact, Bulgari commissioned a whole mystery novel to be written called *The Bulgari Connection.*
- *Street-level promotion.* Companies have hired actors and actresses to walk in busy areas and ask passersby to take a snapshot of them using their new camera phone. Hopefully the picture takers are impressed and tell others about the new camera phone.
- *Celebrity endorsements.* Michael Jordan's endorsements gave a boost to Nike shoes, McDonald's, Hanes underwear, and Rayovac batteries. Ex-Senator Bob Dole's surprising endorsement of Viagra put Viagra on the nation's mind.
- *Body advertising.* College kids agreed to paste Dunkin' Donuts logos on their foreheads during an NCAA basketball tournament.

What is the main communication challenge?

The major challenge today is getting people's attention. Consumers are pressed for time, and many work hard to avoid advertising messages. The main challenge is to find new ways to capture attention and position a brand in the consumers' mind. Public relations and word-of-mouth marketing are playing a growing role within the marketing mix to build and maintain brands.

There is a great deal of hype about integrated marketing communications. What is the status of this subject today?

In the past, we taught separate courses on advertising, sales promotion, public relations, and other communication tools.

Each student became a specialist in one of these areas, remaining ignorant of the other tools and having a tendency to defend the primacy of her tool. Within companies, the advertising person always received the biggest budget for marketing communication (leaving out the sales force), and the others would fight for the crumbs.

Clearly this is not a good situation, especially considering that the effectiveness of different communication tools changes over time. The decision on how much to allocate to the different promotional tools cannot be left to turf battles. Someone must be put in charge. Let's call that person the chief communication officer (CCO). That person should be responsible for everything that communicates anything about the company—not only the standard communication tools, but also corporate dress, office décor, and even the look of the company's trucks.

Today, an increasing number of business schools are teaching marketing communications using an IMC-oriented textbook. First, this prepares the student to understand the role of different communication vehicles. Second, it makes the point that the company's brand and customer message must be communicated consistently through all media. Thus, if a company wants to be known for its high quality, it has to produce high quality and communicate high quality in all of its messages.

Do you see companies as setting their communication budgets optimally?

Marketers develop a certain mindset concerning the most effective communication mix. They will continue the same mix, even when evidence shows diminishing effectiveness. Allocations become frozen, and the chief marketing officer is loath to change the allocation. This would change the power

positions of different communication managers in the organization. Also, it will be done at some risk.

Advertising

Companies continue to spend more money on TV adver-tising, even as the number of channels proliferate and more channel switching takes place. Aren't companies being slow to realize TV advertising effectiveness has fallen?

Companies are still fairly blind to the cataclysmic changes in
the communication marketplace. The days of mass advertising, with its waste and intrusiveness, are passing quickly. I
have advised clients to reduce their TV advertising budgets,
especially mass advertising. Fewer people are watching TV,
many are zapping commercials, and most commercials are
too brief to be effective.

If a country had only a few TV stations, radio stations,
and newspapers, mass marketing would be effective. When
a country, such as the United States, has thousands of TV
stations and radio stations, reaching a mass audience is very
expensive. The few mass audience vehicles are the Super
Bowl or the Olympics. The growing fragmentation of media
audiences requires marketers to shift to target marketing and
even one-to-one marketing. The good news is that this will
reduce wasted media exposures. What good is it to advertise
a cat food on national television if only 20 percent of families
own a cat?

What should advertising agencies do in response to the declining effectiveness of mass advertising?

Advertising agencies can no longer prosper by just creating
ads and choosing media. There are so many new ways to

communicate today. Smart ad agencies will transform themselves into full-service communication agencies. They will work with their clients to choose the best messages and media vehicles, whether these are in the form of ads, press releases, events, sales promotions, sponsorships, direct mail, e-mail, or telesales.

Some advertising agencies have added these communication capabilities—they have created them or networked with public relations firms, sales promotions firms, and direct-marketing firms in a move to becoming total communications firms. Ogilvy called its system Ogilvy Orchestration and promised to deliver integrated marketing communications.

In practice, however, the dominant voice in this comprehensive agency is still that of the agency's advertising group. These agencies still make most of their money from their advertising billings. So how can they be fully objective when advising on the best mix of advertising tools?

Yet advertisers are demanding more communication effectiveness. They want to shift more of their promotion dollars into direct marketing, public relations, and newer promotion tools. Advertising agencies would be wise to transform themselves from being narrowly defined advertising agencies into broad communication agencies.

What is advertising's main limitation?

Traditional advertising works primarily as a monologue. Today's companies would gain considerably by setting up systems that would enable dialogue to take place between the company and its customers and prospects.

Will the Internet become an effective advertising medium?

A few years ago, the CEO of P&G said that he would happily switch a large portion of P&G's huge advertising budget to the Internet if he could find effective ways to do Internet advertising. So far, the Internet has not become a full-blown advertising medium like television, radio, newspapers, or magazines. It is true that the Internet carries banner ads, but they are being opened less than 1 percent of the time. Advertisers are pressing popular web sites to carry skyscraper or pop-up ads, but the web sites see this as risky. Also, consumers can choose to block pop-up ads. Google has developed a system to align paid-for ads next to topics being searched by consumers. For example, if I type "BMW" on Google, the right side of Google's page will show a BMW ad. BMW will quickly learn whether their ad is leading to sales. All said, it is too early to tell how widespread or effective Internet advertising will become.

How can companies effectively reach mass audiences?

Advertisers won't see again the glorious days when they could reach millions of people in the evening with the same TV show or mass magazine. There are three options today: One is to advertise on a number of media channels in the same time slot. Another is to advertise on Super Bowls, the Olympics, and other major worldwide events that attract large audiences. A third is to build a giant database containing the names of people who have the greatest interest in the company's offerings.

Public Relations

Some media analysts call for more spending on public relatons. Do you agree?

I agree. Advertising has been overdone in the past, especially mass advertising with its "hit or miss" quality. PR has been underdone. PR consists of many tools, which I call the PEN-CILS of PR: publications, events, news, community involvement, identity tools, lobbying, and social investments. When a customer sees an ad, she knows it is an ad, and an increasing number of customers are tuning out. PR has a better chance of getting a message through. Furthermore the message can be fresher and more believable. PR is better equipped to create "buzz" about a new product or service. Interest in PR is increasing—witness the title of the recent book by Al and Laura Ries, *The Fall of Advertising and the Rise of PR*.

Sales Promotion

My company used to spend about 70 percent of our promotion dollars on advertising and 30 percent on sales promotion. Now we are spending 70 percent on sales promotion. Are we spending too much on sales promotion?

Your company is not alone in experiencing sales promotion "inflation." Most companies have been increasing their expenditures on both consumer and trade promotion relative to advertising. There are many reasons for this. First, advertising works much more slowly than sales promotion. Sales promotions give incentives to "buy now." "This week only: XYZ laptops for half price!" Sales promotions appeal to managers who are desperate to meet their quarterly targets. Understandably, managers want to shift their funds to faster-acting sales tools. Second, TV advertising is becoming less effective as a result of shorter and more clustered TV commercials, zapping, TIVO, and other factors.

But here is the rub: Most sales promotions have a negative impact on brand image. They cheapen rather than build the brand. When the company continuously offers discounts, gifts, rebates, and other incentives, these detract from the brand's specialness. If one listens to automobile ads today, one could easily believe that there is a fire sale on every car. Don't buy the car for its virtues; buy the car because the price has been lowered.

I remember being asked by a manager at the Leo Burnett Advertising agency whether sales promotion is excessive when it reaches 30 percent of the total budget for advertising and promotion. The advertising manager, of course, was hoping to get evidence that companies are hurting their brand by spending too much on sales promotion. Given to-day's 70 percent budget for promotion, I would argue that companies would be wise to downsize their sales promotion budget and put the money to better use through other forms of promotion or by improving service, developing new or better products, or simply reducing their list prices.

How should the sales promotion budget be divided between trade and consumer promotion?

Trade promotion (trade allowances, gifts, extra cases, and so on) are used to secure more and better shelf space, point-of-purchase display space, and better retailer cooperation. The trade expects them—no, demands them. The trade makes considerable profit on the manufacturer's trade promotion money. Efforts to cut down on trade promotions often result in much less trade support. If anything, trade promotion is growing relative to consumer promotion.

Companies have more control over their budgeting for consumer promotions. Even here, however, businesses need to assess these promotions' effectiveness. The worst case is consumer promotions to which only your present customers respond. This amounts to giving an unnecessary subsidy to your present customers. The next worst case is consumer promotions that attract some new customers, but mainly deal-prone customers who are not likely to buy the product at the regular price. The sales lift is one time only, and the sales promotion is probably not profitable given the cost of mounting the promotion. The best case, which happens much less often, is where the promotion attracts new triers who like the product and switch to it. This happens primarily when the product is really better than competitors' products. Given this mix of cases, it is not surprising that most sales promotions lose money for the company.

What is the best way to improve the use of sales promotion?

Hire a sales promotion agency. Don't do it yourself. Sales promotion agencies have designed many promotions and are in a better position to know what works and what doesn't work. We outsource marketing research and advertising. Why not outsource sales promotion to the experts?

Sales Management and Selling

What is the relationship between the marketing department and the sales force?

In theory, the sales force should report to the marketing vice president because she is responsible for marketing strategy. The sales force is one of several marketing tools. In practice, however, the sales force normally reports to the sales vice president, who is independent of the marketing vice president and who typically forms and fights for his own budget. In many case, the sales force is a larger budget item than marketing and is more crucial to the company's short run success in delivering today's sales. In fact, marketing departments were originally small and were set up primarily to carry out certain functions that would help the salespeople call on the right customers at the right time with the right value proposition.

It is critical to a company's success that the marketing department and the salespeople work well together and support each other. Although they have different ideas on how to spend the total budget, they must co-plan strategy and tactics.

The role of marketing is to identify opportunities, build distinctive brands, and generate demand. The role of sales is to convert demand into orders. Sales must participate in the setting of strategy; otherwise sales might not buy in. Marketing must recognize sales as an internal customer and do its best to satisfy this "customer."

Should salespeople receive some training in marketing?

Salespeople will be more effective if they understand more about marketing and how marketing plans are formulated. They should understand how marketers do market research, forecasting, product testing, and advertising. This exposure can be achieved through training sessions and occasional marketing assignments. This will bring the two departments into a closer understanding of each other's roles and responsibilities.

I believe that sales should have a strong input into the marketing planning process. Salespeople need to feel that the marketing plan makes sense. Actually, the first task of marketing is to sell the marketing plan to the sales force, and this is more easily done if the sales force had some input into the marketing planning process.

What is the best system for compensating the sales force?

There is no best system. Salespeople can be compensated by straight salary, commissions, bonuses, or some mix of these.

Straight salary is appropriate when salespeople have more routine tasks to perform, such as collecting market intelligence and receiving, processing, and delivering orders. Commission systems make more sense when the challenge is to find new customers and convince them to buy your goods. Commission systems attract more aggressive and independent sales types who like to be challenged and who will work harder in order to get more pay. Companies may pay bonuses for superior performances. Most sales compensation plans are based on a combination of salary and commission.

The best salespeople far outperform the average salespeople in a sales force. How much more should they be paid?

I favor paying a lot more to the top earners. If they sell four times as much, paying them three times as much is still profitable for the company. I remember a brilliant new IBM salesperson who sold his quota in the first few months. The compensation system was such that he could not earn more by selling more. He argued that the company should give him more targets so that he could earn more money. They balked, saying that he shouldn't earn more than the CEO of the company. This was stupid! If the salesperson earned more, the CEO would also earn more. The salesperson left and started his own company. Incidentally, his name is Ross Perot and he founded EDS.

What is the future of salespeople in business-to-business marketing?

E-business threatens to reduce the number of sales jobs, especially in the B2B world. Purchasing agents tell me that the Internet provides them with fairly complete and detailed information about different vendors' products. Purchasing agents can go to e-hubs where they can make quick price and feature comparisons rather than taking up their time with salespeople's presentations. They don't need or want visits from salespeople who simply repeat the product information that is available on the Internet.

We will still need sales forces to sell complex equipment and projects. These salespeople will need more than communication and persuasion skills. Their success will require them to understand each customer's business and be able to add value as consultants to the customer. This is called "consultative selling."

Sponsorships

Do you think companies should divert some money from advertising to sponsorship?

If a company feels that its paid advertising isn't very effective, it should seriously consider shifting some money to public relations and other areas. Sponsorship, one tool of public relations, can take several forms—sponsoring events, places, persons, ideas, or causes—that attract attention from the right audiences. Usually the company can find one or more of these platforms where it can draw special attention. The main problem is that the company must find some way to measure the impact of its sponsorship investments. Another problem is that it is not easy to terminate certain sponsorships once they are started. The audience will wonder why the company could not afford to continue the particular sponsorship.

Buzz Marketing

What's your opinion of so-called buzz marketing?

Buzz marketing, the effort to generate business by word of mouth, will increase substantially. Marketers have improved their ability to identify influentials, opinion leaders, and mavens and reach them early so that they can do the work of spreading the word about a distinct product or service.

Media

How has new media changed consumer behavior?

New media have been a boon to consumers who are pressed for time. Consumers can do home-based shopping through catalogs, direct mail, the telephone, television shopping shows, and the Internet. They can do their banking on the phone or by Internet. They can order their groceries on their laptop for home delivery.

Industrial companies are conducting more of their business using intranets, internets, and extranets. They use intranets for internal communication within the company; the Internet for informing, selling, and buying; and extranets for conducting transactions with their suppliers and dealers. We have passed from the Industrial Age to the Information Age, thanks to electronic markets.

Which media will be the winners in the coming ten years?

Here are my predictions:

- Newspapers will continue to decline in circulation. Many young people have stopped reading newspapers.
- TV will continue to attract viewers, but those viewers will be paying less attention to commercials. Two million households now have TIVOs, and it is predicted that 20 percent of all households will have TIVOs by 2008.
- The use of radio will increase, if for no other reason than that traffic is getting more congested and people

are spending more time in their cars. This is offset to the extent that car drivers listen to tapes or CDs instead of their radio.

- Magazines will increase in number because they can be highly targeted and develop loyal subscribers who are interested in the particular content.
- Billboards may increase in impact because people are spending more time in their cars because of traffic congestion.
- The Internet, e-mail, and chat rooms will grow considerably in importance as the younger generation, who have been raised on the Internet, grow older and represent a greater percentage of consumer purchases.

PART 4

Marketing Planning

Should marketing plans use the same format? What should that format be?

I am in favor of using a standard marketing planning format within each company. This enables senior management to compare the different plans easily. Also, it provides an orderly way to think about effective marketing.

A marketing plan should progress through six steps: situational analysis, objectives, strategy, tactics, budget, and controls.

- *Situational analysis.* Here the company examines the *macro forces* (economics, political-legal, social-cultural, and technological) and the *players* (the company, competitors, distributors, and suppliers) in its environment. The company carries out a SWOT analysis (strengths, weaknesses, opportunities, and threats). This section should conclude with an identification of the main issues facing the business unit.
- *Objectives.* After identifying its best opportunities from its situational analysis, the company ranks them, defines the target markets, and sets goals and a timetable for achieving them. The company also sets objectives with respect to stakeholders, company reputation, technology, and other matters of concern.

- *Strategies*. Any goal can be pursued in a variety of ways. It is the job of strategy to choose the most effective course of action for attaining its objectives.
- *Tactics*. The strategy must be spelled out in great detail in terms of the 4Ps and the actions that will be taken in calendar time by the specific individuals who are to carry out the plan.
- *Budget*. The company's planned actions and activities involve costs, which add up to the budget that it needs to achieve its objectives.
- *Controls*. The company must establish review periods and metrics that will reveal whether it is making progress toward its plan. When performance lags, the company must revise its objectives, strategies, or actions to correct the situation.

How can you assess whether a marketing plan is a good one?

My experience with marketing plans is that most of them are poorly done. Some are overloaded with numbers and ads, but lack a compelling strategy. Or the strategy is there, but the tactics seem unrelated to the strategy. Or the targets are unrealistic. Or the budget is unrealistic. Or the controls are not adequate for feedback and plan revision.

No marketing plan is guaranteed to work, but poor plans are almost guaranteed not to work.

What is the difference between a business plan and a marketing plan?

Companies differ in their use of these terms. Some companies start with a marketing plan and then turn it into a business plan. The business plan brings in plans for purchasing, production, finance and, so on. Other companies use the term *business plan* from the beginning. However, the marketing plan should be the start of any business plan.

I sometimes call the marketing plan a *battle plan*. Your plan should give you confidence that you will win the war before you engage in the first battle. If you aren't introducing something that is better, newer, faster, or cheaper, you shouldn't be in the market. Yet no battle plan survives the first battle. It will need constant revision as the battle progresses. You may have to redesign your "plane" while you are in the "air."

Some people say that a marketing plan is obsolete as soon as it is finished, because conditions are always changing. Is this true?

A company doesn't need to change its objectives and strategies when conditions change. The first line of defense is to change its tactics and budget. If this doesn't work, it will change its strategy. If this doesn't work, it will have to change its objectives.

The most important thing about planning is not the plan. As Eisenhower observed: "In preparing for battle I have always found that plans are useless but planning is indispensable." Planning forces you to think deeply and futuristically in a more systematic manner.

Marketing Research

Do you believe that all marketing decisions require market research?

No. But no company should make big decisions without information about customers, competitors, and channels. If the company is developing a new product, it should use focus groups and surveys to help estimate the size of the market opportunity. After the product is launched, data on the characteristics of the early buyers and their post-use attitudes are needed. This information helps the company learn and fine-tune its market targets and marketing programs over time. I view market research as the foundational element of modern marketing practice.

Do other company managers respect market research?

Some don't. They have strong prior convictions, and when the research is contrary to their expectations, they prefer to go with their gut feeling.

It is interesting, however, that top companies like Procter & Gamble (P&G) and General Mills want their brand managers to do fresh research each year to track what customers think of the category and competitive brands. P&G executives actually criticize brand managers who spend too little money on marketing research.

Companies tend to spend one-half of 1 percent on research and 99.5 percent on promotion, when they would be better off spending 1½ or 2 percent on research to better target and fine-tune their advertising and promotion.

What tools—quantitative or qualitative—will contribute more to market success?

This question is reminiscent of the old debate between "nose counters" who favored quantitative techniques and "head shrinkers" who favored qualitative techniques for understanding the market. Quantitative marketing tools are moving beyond scientific sampling to include perceptual mapping, conjoint analysis, market simulation, expert systems, and other such tools. At the same time, qualitative tools must be used to understand buyer behavior that can't be modeled at the quantitative level, such as deeper needs, perceptions, and preferences. It is not either/or when it comes to quantitative versus qualitative techniques in marketing.

How dependable are focus groups as a way of testing consumers' ideas concerning a new product?

Focus groups provide interesting ideas and perspectives. They should almost always be part of assessing new products and projects. Companies often run several focus groups to get the perspectives of different groups of customers. At the same time, running several focus groups is not a substitute for conducting a larger market survey to get a more representative sampling of opinion.

What do you think about the effectiveness of online surveys and market research?

Online market research presents endless opportunities for learning about customers, markets and market segments, competitors, channels of distribution, and trends. Never before has so much rich information been available to companies for the asking.

Many companies have appointed consumer and dealer panels whose members are ready to meet online to give their opinions of proposed products and ads. However, the findings should be treated as exploratory, inasmuch as the respondents are a nonrandom sample. The findings have the same limitations as do those coming from a focus group.

PART 5

Marketing Organization

What role should the marketing department play in a company?

I would like the marketing department to drive the business strategy surrounding any product or service. All business strategy has to start with the marketplace, and who better understands the marketplace than the members of the marketing department? The marketing department presumably buys market research and in principle has the best understanding of the behavior of customers, competitors, and channel members.

This being said, too many marketing departments do not play this role. They spend most of their energy and budget trying to sell what the company has decided to make. Therefore, they have become promotion departments, not marketing departments. They are 1P marketers (promotion) rather than 4P marketers (product, price, place, and promotion). In the process, marketing has been marginalized.

How can companies become more customer-centric?

The company's CEO needs to manage a whole process—spread over a number of years—to move the company to deep customer-centricity. Here are the steps:

1. The CEO must convince senior management of the need to and benefits of becoming customer-centered.
2. Appoint a senior marketing officer and marketing task force.
3. Get outside help and guidance.
4. Change the company's reward and measurement systems.
5. Hire strong marketing talent.
6. Develop strong in-house marketing training programs.
7. Install a modern marketing planning system.
8. Establish an annual marketing excellence recognition program.
9. Shift from a department focus to a process and outcome focus.
10. Empower the employees to be "innovators."

I would recommend following the prescription in Sandra Vandermerve's new book, *Breaking Through: Implementing Customer Focus in Enterprises.*

What happens to the marketing department when everyone in the company becomes customer-focused?

The marketing department will not become useless even if every employee magically becomes customer-oriented. It will still need to carry out three functions. First, the department will hire, house, train, and evaluate the marketing specialists. Second, the department will be responsible for marketing strategy development. Third, the department will be responsible for integrating all the customer-impinging forces so that the company's offerings, products, and services are coherently presented to customers.

Do you believe that the best way to organize companies is by functions?

Companies have been traditionally organized by function, with the result that each department acts to maximize its own interest, not the company's overall interest. Too many walls arise between departments that impede their collaborative planning. In response, companies are now identifying their basic business processes and reengineering them so that they operate faster and more efficiently. Each process is headed by a process leader, who works with a multifunctional team to achieve desired outcomes. Marketing and sales people are members of these various process teams.

Name a weakness of marketing departments that irritates you.

Marketing departments tend to develop a set budget and allocation pattern that persists year after year. Each manager wants at least the same amount of funds as she spent last year plus some. Few raise questions about radically shifting the budget toward more productive uses of the money. Yet it is vitally important to make periodic adjustments in budgets to reflect strong changes in the economy, customer behavior, and competition.

What are the challenges facing the chief marketing officer in a company?

The CMO of a company must win the confidence of his CEO and work well with the heads of other departments. He must ultimately show that his strategies and investments have created profitable growth. The CMO must wrestle with the following problems:

1. How can we justify a larger marketing budget?
2. How can we find new product opportunities that will deliver profitable growth?
3. Should we shift advertising money into newer communication media such as PR, direct marketing, event marketing, and the Internet?
4. Should we enter into newer distribution channels?
5. How can marketing and sales work better together?
6. What new skills does the marketing department need?
7. Should marketing be organized by skills, product groups, market segments, channels, or geography?

How have marketing departments become 1P marketers (promotion primarily)? Why has this happened?

The work done by people in the marketing department varies with a product's stage in the life cycle. In the case of new product launches, marketing prepares a comprehensive 4P work plan: choosing the product features and benefits to emphasize, pricing the product, placing it in distribution, and arranging for extensive promotion. But with mature products, most of marketing's energy is consumed by promotion. Given that most products in a company's portfolio are mature products, most of the work in marketing departments is promotional work.

The heavy promotional focus and intensity is not only the result of so many mature products, but also the result of growing hypercompetition and sameness among brands. Too many companies are intent upon copying the successful products of other companies, leading to a sameness in brand offerings.

Promotional focus is further intensified by economic recession, where companies are competing for survival, not profitability. Promotional spending is at a minimum in periods of shortage and moves to a maximum in periods of product surfeit.

A further problem arises in the choice of promotional tools. We know that the productivity of different promotional tools—TV commercials, radio commercials, magazine ads, sponsorships—changes over time. For example, increasing traffic congestion means that people will spend more time in cars, and as a result, radio commercials will increase in listenership. But in spite of the changing productivities of different promotion tools, companies tend to perpetuate the same promotional mix year after year.

Why? First, because this is safer for the market planners. How can they be criticized for repeating what worked in the past? There is much more risk in trying something new that may not work at all.

Second, changing the promotional mix calls for altering staff and agencies. For example, if a company decided to switch half of its advertising budget to public relations or e-marketing, its advertising staff and agency would have to be reduced. Terminating people is not pleasant.

Third, companies generally don't do a good job of tracking the changing productivities of different marketing tools. They need to establish better metrics.

All said, much of a marketing department's energy is consumed in promotion work rather than in innovating product, price, and channel ideas.

This further confirms the picture that some CEOs have of marketing: that it is equivalent to promotion and selling. The other three P's—product, price, and place, or distribution—get obscured by the company's relentless need to sell what it is already producing.

What additional skills will be needed in marketing departments to be effective?

Traditional marketing departments need to be skilled at market research, advertising, sales promotion, and sales management. In today's e-world, additional skills are needed in the marketing department. I would list the following skills:

- Brand-building and positioning skills
- Database management and data-mining skills
- Customer relationship management skills
- Customer profitability measurement skills
- Public relations and "buzz marketing" skills
- Event management and experiential marketing skills
- Direct mail, catalog marketing, and telemarketing skills

Does marketing alone set the business strategy?

Although I often say that marketing should be the driver of business strategy, I don't mean that all the decisions are to be made in the marketing department. The product must be codeveloped and codesigned by marketers working with scientists, engineers, and manufacturing and purchasing people. The price must be co-decided with the finance people. The choice and management of distribution channels requires marketers to work with the company's lawyers and finance people. And the proposed promotion budget requires the acquiescence of the finance people.

My main point is that the 4Ps must be consistent, namely, inspired by a dominant idea about the distinctive value to be delivered to meet the needs of a distinct group of buyers in a superior way. The 4Ps must be designed to deliver this value in a consistent and compelling way.

Does the CEO have any role to play in marketing?

The CEO should play the role of chief marketing officer. His role can be critical in selling large business-to-business projects such as large computer systems or power stations. Part of Lou Gerstner's success in revitalizing IBM is the result of his spending 30 percent of his time meeting customers. In GE's case, ex-CEO Jack Welch recognized the importance of selling from the top. He changed the name of the head of each major GE division from vice president to CEO. Now GE has thirteen CEOs to call on senior executives in customer companies. Jack Welch personally called on over a hundred of GE's major customers each year.

Is the work of a marketing department to be increasingly outsourced?

Today, much of a marketing department's work is outsourced. The company uses an advertising agency to do its advertising, a sales promotion agency to do its sales promotion, and a market research firm to do its market research. Companies that are exporting for the first time often hire an export management firm to carry out this work. Smaller companies may outsource all their marketing to a marketing firm.

What should be the relationship between marketing and finance?

Marketing people bear some of the blame for tensions with the finance department. The finance director wants assurance that marketing funds are being spent in a profitable way. Marketing people often fail to supply hard numbers to back their proposals—and to financially account for results. Granted, projecting the return on a proposed advertising campaign or sales promotion is difficult. But marketing must move to more financial accountability. The finance directors, of course, also must open their minds to a better understanding of how marketing works—that its impact is cumulative and that many items that finance directors want to treat as expenses are more properly viewed as investments.

What is the employee's role in carrying out the company's marketing strategy and goals?

A company must develop a clear and compelling strategy and set of policies and communicate them effectively to every employee. One policy should be, "the customer comes first." Every employee must internalize this message and behave accordingly. The employees in companies such as the Four Seasons hotels or the Container Store always think "the customer is always right" and act on it. This goes a long way toward building loyal customers.

How can a company motivate its employees to go the extra few yards for the customer?

Think of your employees as you think of your customers— they are internal customers; they have needs and wants. By meeting their needs and wants better, you hopefully can increase your employees' satisfaction and therefore their performance.

In former times, zero-sum thinking prevailed, in that manufacturers thought that they would make the most money by paying the least to employees, suppliers, and distributors. But this led to poorer inputs and outputs and lots of employee and partner turnover. Smart companies today practice positive-sum thinking and treat their suppliers, employees, and distributors as partners who are motivated to deliver superior value. "Win-win-win" thinking will prevail over "I win, you lose" thinking.

Hal Rosenbluth, who runs a major national travel agency, wrote a best-selling book with the surprising title

The Customer Comes Second. In service businesses such as hotels, restaurants, and banks, a case can be made that satisfying the employees is the company's number one job. Bill Marriott, Jr., says that if he has managed to satisfy his employees, they will satisfy the customers, the customers will come back to Marriott hotels, and the stockholders will be rewarded. So Marriott and other service leaders put a lot of emphasis on meeting the needs of the employees. This task has been called *internal marketing* for the reason that we are trying to sense, serve, and satisfy an internal market, the employees.

Leaders can learn the needs of their internal customers in a number of ways. John Welch instituted the Work-Out approach, where his division heads had to listen to their employees' ideas and proposals for improvement and get back to them with answers. Other companies periodically provide forms for employees to rate their bosses. I think bosses would learn a great deal about their workers' needs by getting into the trenches and assuming a worker's role. One week a year, the senior managers at McDonald's and at Disney leave their offices and take up the job of cooking hamburgers, taking tickets, and meeting employees and customers.

Leaders have to articulate not just a plan but an inspiring goal. They must state the goal not only in financial terms, but in social benefit terms. A fertilizer company does not just make fertilizer; its aspiration should be to help feed the world's hungry, to put an end to world starvation. I subscribe to the incentive value of formulating lofty goals.

A major task of the leader is to get everyone in the company to see the customer as the center of their universe. The workers must recognize that the company doesn't pay them; the customers do. Senior management must spell out to each department how its members affect customer satisfaction and retention, and what it costs the company when a customer is lost.

PART 6

Marketing Control

While overall productivity is on the rise, marketing productivity has been on the decline. What's gone wrong? Can marketing ROI be measured?

Although companies can generally measure the expected payoff from capital expenditures, they have done a poor job of measuring even the post-hoc payoff from marketing expenditures. Granted, marketing payoffs are subject to more uncertainty because of competitive moves and exogenous factors. But, hopefully, some progress can be made. We are recognizing that measuring only communication effects (such as awareness and preference) is not enough. We need measures of sales and ROI impact. The good news is that several researchers are working on measuring marketing ROI. I would recommend reading Tim Ambler's *Marketing and the Bottom Line*, Guy Powell's *Return of Marketing Investment*, and Jim Lenskold's *Marketing ROI: The Path to Campaign, Customer, and Corporate Profitability*.

What tools can marketers use to show the impact of their marketing programs on the bottom line?

Marketing costs are high and rising. Yet marketing is still hard pressed to present measures of the impact of marketing on ROI or shareholder value. Most companies still don't know the profitability of individual customers, market segments, geographical areas, marketing channels, or order sizes. Most companies cannot measure the impact of their image advertising campaigns or sponsorships on their bottom line.

Some progress is being made by using activity-based costing to measure all the resources being consumed by each customer, segment, channel, and territory. The costs can then be subtracted from the revenues to determine the profitability of each marketing entity.

The ideal way to assess the profit impact of marketing programs is to conduct marketing experiments in matched territories or segments. Today some companies are using split cable to send different messages or offers to comparable groups and note the difference in response. Measurement nevertheless remains difficult for image campaigns because of the delayed effects.

What metrics can companies use to judge marketing performance?

Metrics should be developed as a joint project between the marketing department and the finance department. If the marketing department took complete responsibility, there would be suspicion that the methodology chosen was biased. If the finance department took complete responsibility, marketing would be distrustful. When both departments sign off on the metrics, it will gain credence. In addition, the finance department will be a beneficiary because it must ultimately use the metrics to guide the allocation of funds to requests coming from the marketing department.

Among the metrics most often used are market share, brand awareness, customer satisfaction, relative product quality, customer perceived value, customer loyalty, and customer loss rate.

Do companies pay enough attention to measuring customer satisfaction?

The majority of companies pay more attention to the increase in their market share than to the level of customer satisfaction. This is wrong. Customer satisfaction and customer perceived value are key to building company profits. The higher the level of customer satisfaction, the higher the customer loyalty. The benefits of loyal customers are many. Acquiring new customers costs five to ten times more than satisfying and keeping existing customers. A 5 percent reduction in customer loss may increase a company's profitability by between 25 and 85 percent, depending on the industry. Furthermore, a customer's profitability tends to increase the longer the customer stays with the company.

PART 7

Marketing Areas of Application

Consumer Packaged Goods

Consumer packaged goods (CPG) companies still rely heavily on TV advertising and sales promotion. Does this make sense?

I believe that CPG firms waste a lot of money on national advertising. It is much harder to reach a mass audience today, given the proliferation of TV channels, the zapping that occurs, and the fact that people are increasingly busy and are shifting their recreational patterns away from TV. Yet brand managers fear that if they reduce their expenditures on national advertising, they will put their brand's popularity at risk. Spending a lot on national advertising is safe, since no one can measure its rate of return and no brand manager can be blamed for cutting the ad budget.

Trade promotions are no better. One estimate is that only 18 percent of trade promotions are profitable. While promotions have the advantage of moving the goods out of the stores, most manufacturers wish they could eliminate or reduce trade promotions.

I would like to see more money allocated to micromarketing activities.

A company should focus its spending on the geographical and demographic markets where it is strongest rather than hitting the whole country with ads. I would like to see more done to build a customer database that is data mined to detect new patterns of behavior and new segment opportunities. I would like to see greater use of direct marketing, including direct mail, telemarketing, and the use of the Internet.

Retail Marketing

How can major manufacturers handle the growing power of mega-retailers to set terms and conditions for carrying their products?

There is an intensifying battle between manufacturers and mega-retailers. Power is shifting to giant mass merchandisers and category killers that unilaterally decide which companies' products they will carry. Some giant retailers even dictate the design, pricing, and packaging of the manufacturers' products. Manufacturers will need skill in demonstrating and documenting the profits that the mega-retailer will make if it carries that manufacturer's product.

Will online marketing make some retail stores superfluous?

The Internet will be a curse to some retail sectors. There will be a decline in the number of travel agents, insurance agents, stockbrokers, car salespeople, bookstores, and music stores, to name a few. Today customers can order large appliances, furniture, home food delivery, and even automobiles over the Internet. Store-based retailers have already been hit by the growth of catalog ordering and will be further hit by the growth of online ordering. Store managers need to start figuring out how to make their stores more interesting to customers. Instead of simply carrying products, they must think about how to design a more satisfying store experience.

Shopping malls, by contrast, will be less hurt by online selling. Shopping malls offer restaurants, movie theatres, places to congregate, and places to see and touch goods that one would never know about from the Internet. Yet shopping malls in some cities are oversaturated, and the older ones are declining relative to the newer ones. Also, shopping malls must take cognizance of the virtual malls coming on the Internet, such as Wal-Mart, and Amazon.

What strategies can small retailers use to compete with large organizations like Wal-Mart?

Smaller retailers that face competition from Wal-Mart and other mass merchandisers have two major recourses. One is to move toward specialty or superspecialty merchandising, meaning that the retailer offers a deeper product assortment and expertise to a more focused set of customers. The second is for the retailer to distinguish itself on a customer-service, customer-intimate basis. The small retailer cannot compete on cost or price, because Wal-Mart is more operationally excellent. But the small retailer can outperform Wal-Mart on intimately knowing its customers and serving and even anticipating their needs.

Small-Business Marketing

What can small businesses do to improve their marketing effectiveness?

Managers of small businesses can turn to a lot of resources to learn about effective marketing. They can read a marketing textbook or trade-oriented books that describe and illustrate marketing theory and practice. They can attend the short courses on marketing offered by many business schools. They can hire a marketing professor to serve as a part-time consultant. They can arrange for class projects under the professor. They can solicit marketing ideas from their advertising agency. Ultimately they might spot an excellent professional marketer and put him on a retainer.

Small and medium-size businesses can use low-cost market research (focus groups) and low-cost promotion (leaflets, flyers, and public relations). There is a series of books on "guerrilla marketing" that are full of tips on "street" tactics for building awareness and gaining product trial.

Small companies can win against large companies in four ways:

1. Becoming a specialist in a particular niche
2. Being more flexible in designing the offering
3. Providing superior service
4. Personalizing interactions with buyers

Direct Marketing

What can be done to improve response rates in direct marketing?

A low response rate in direct marketing is the result, when it occurs, of using the wrong mailing lists, having inadequate information on prospects and customers, and having an unrefined system of scoring prospects. Companies that have developed an information-intense customer database and have mastered precision analytics can achieve higher response rates with fewer mailings.

Do you think direct marketing can be overdone, taking the form of a lot of "junk" mail?

If direct marketing is carried out perfectly, the right people will be receiving the promotional information and welcoming it. A direct marketer does not want to make an offer to a person who has little or no interest in the product or service. Mass marketing is intrinsically untargeted because it assaults the eyes and ears of many uninterested people. Direct marketing is "directed" to those who have a potentially high interest in the product. Yet if our mailing lists are poor or our products are inappropriate, we will irritate those people who receive the messages. They will call this "junk" mail or "junk" phone calls and clamor for their regulation. Some regulation will occur sooner or later to prevent abuses, but "non-junk" direct marketing is still possible in principle.

With the advent of the Internet, are physical mailings likely to continue?

Physical mailings will continue into the foreseeable future. U.S. citizens continue to receive a large number of catalogs that sell everything from clothes to furniture to electronics. These catalogs provide superior color, and people like to browse them. Some catalogs, of course, will go online eventually, especially B2B catalogs that rely more on technical description. We will also continue to receive many fund-raising letters and brochures promoting plays and musical performances. The question of what types of physical mailings will persist and what types will gravitate to e-mail, faxes, and the Internet needs further study.

Do you favor collecting information about individual customers?

Marketing has moved from working on mass markets to targeting market segments, then market niches, and now individual customers. Thanks to checkout scanners, call centers, and digital software and hardware, companies can increasingly capture information about individuals for the purpose of improving their targeting of offerings, services, and messages. Using predictive analytics, the company can do a better job of targeting the best prospects. To that extent, I favor it. But the concerns about privacy may lead to an organized customer backlash objecting to the loss of individual privacy.

Customers are rushing to protect their privacy from the intrusiveness of "junk" mail, "junk" telephone calls, and e-mail spam. I don't blame them, and I have personally opted out from receiving unsolicited communications. This will reduce company sales somewhat, but consumers will gain in the process. Opting out is not all bad because there is a countermovement toward "permission marketing." IBM, for example, dropped its practice of bombarding managers with all kinds of promotions and moved toward asking each manager (1) what she would like to hear about, (2) how she would like to be reached (mail, phone, fax, e-mail), and (3) how frequently she is willing to be contacted.

Loyalty Marketing

How can companies build more customer loyalty?

A company can build customer loyalty in a number of ways. Customers can be given points or awards based on how much they purchase. The best examples of this are the airlines' frequent flyer programs and hotels' counterpart programs. The company can sponsor events that deliver some value for its customers to keep them interested. Harley-Davidson's rallies provide an excellent example. The company can lend its customers equipment or software that they will have to surrender if they switch to another vendor. Thus McKesson Robbins supplies computers and proprietary software to retail pharmacists to make it easier for them to order replacement stock. They would have to return this equipment if they switched. Many companies are creating membership clubs to increase customer loyalty—clubs such as Swatch Club, the Rolling Stones Fan Club, the Pampers Parenting Institute, Casa Buitoni, the Harley Owners Group (HOG), and the Volkswagen Club.

What makes an effective frequency program for building loyalty?

Effective loyalty programs must be simple to understand and use. There are no hidden clauses or exceptions or disappointments. They must be backed up by excellent goods and services; otherwise the program won't last. Loyalty programs have their place, although when all competitors adopt them, the companies end up in the same market stalemate as before, but with higher costs. Many airline passengers carry the cards of several airlines and still choose flights based on schedule and cost rather than the loyalty program.

Companies try to create loyal customers. But often they give a larger reward to new customers than to loyal customers. Is this right?

Companies have the perverse habit of rewarding new customers with lower costs while saddling their loyal customers with higher costs. For example, my auto insurance company offers lower rates to entice new customers, while I have to pay higher rates even though I have no accidents on my record during the many years of "being loyal." The right approach is to reward your customers for each year they renew and have no accidents.

Will loyalty lessen as a result of the Internet making competitors' offers and prices more visible?

The Internet poses an irony in that until the Internet, businesses were moving toward loyalty marketing. They were identifying their best customers, offering frequency reward schemes, and implementing relationship-building measures. Along came the Internet, and it brought many buyers back to a *transaction* mentality. Namely, it is so easy to price-shop on the Internet that the notion of remaining loyal to any single supplier is weakening. My assessment is that loyalty marketing is made harder by the growing use of the Internet.

What is the core idea of stakeholder marketing?

Companies can no longer operate as self-contained, fully capable units without dedicated partners. At one time, the Ford Motor Company grew its own wool for the seat covers of its cars, made its own steel and window glass, and practiced a high level of vertical integration. Today, companies are de-verticalizing. Each company decides what it should make and what it should buy from the outside. Outsourcing is much more popular now. Companies are becoming increasingly dependent on their employees, their suppliers, their distributors and dealers, and their advertising agency. This dependence involves some loss of company freedom of action, but it increases the prospect of higher productivity and profitability. The key is for the company to form close relationships with its stakeholders. The company needs to build a network of partners that all gain from their joint strategy and behavior. Mutual trust is the bond. Selecting good partners and motivating them is the key to stakeholder marketing.

Hasn't customer relationship marketing always been practiced?

Customer relationship marketing has a long history in business-to-business (B2B) marketing. Many business marketers have a direct relationship with their customers and build many bridges of relationship. Consumer marketers have less immediate contact with their ultimate customers; their contact is through intermediaries such as distributors and retailers. Some consumer companies—such as Harley-Davidson and Apple Computer—have built strong, loyal customers through the use of relationship marketing ideas.

CRM and Database Marketing

What do sales and marketing professionals need to be aware of when considering making a major CRM investment?

Customer relationship management (CRM) is one of the most promising new marketing developments in recent years. The more a company knows about its customers and prospects, the more effectively it can compete. At least, that is the theory.

CRM was sold as a technological breakthrough that would enable greater precision in identifying prospects and making offers. Many companies invested millions of dollars to gather data, only to find that the data missed a lot of important variables and, worse, the company's people were not customer-oriented or customer-organized to begin with. The performance of CRM investments in recent years has been poor, with somewhere between 40 and 60 percent of companies reporting disappointing results. When you add new technology to an old organization, you only end up with an expensive old organization! Before any company invests in

CRM, it first needs to create a customer-driven culture in the organization. Then the personnel in all the company departments can use the database to learn things about customers.

So the challenge is to know when CRM is an appropriate investment and how to implement it successfully. CRM makes the most sense in data-rich industries such as banking, credit cards, insurance, and telecommunications. It makes the least sense in mass consumer markets selling low-priced goods.

In deciding whether to invest in an expensive CRM system, consider what the Royal Bank of Canada did. It asked the CRM vendor, the Siebel Company, for four estimates:

1. What will the system cost?
2. How long will it be before the system will be operational?
3. In how many months will the incremental sales above baseline cover the initial system investment?
4. What is the long-run ROI that we will get from this system?

I like the following quotes about CRM. Steve Silver says, "CRM is not a software package. It's not a database. It's not a call center or a Web site. It's not a loyalty program, a customer service program, a customer acquisition program, or a win-back program. CRM is an entire philosophy." And Edmund Thompson of the Gartner Group says, "A CRM program is typically 45 percent dependent on the right executive leadership, 40 percent on project management implementation, and 15 percent on technology." These comments sound right to me.

What kinds of companies will benefit most from using CRM?

CRM is a great system, but it is not for every company. It is being overhyped, and some companies will regret adopting it. It won't work unless the company is customer-centered to begin with.

The downside of CRM is that collecting, updating, and managing individual customer information is very expensive. Much information, such as addresses and job positions, becomes obsolete each year. The company has to buy expensive hardware and software. The company needs to hire experienced data analysts to do data mining. All these costs are not worth it for companies selling low-unit-cost items or selling items that people purchase once in a lifetime.

CRM is highly suited to B2B marketing. Most B2B companies know a great deal about individual customers. CRM makes sense for companies that gather a lot of individual data, such as banks, credit card companies, telecoms, and insurance companies. Yet many B2C companies have built customer databases. Dell's sales to individual customers are recorded in its database, and Dell knows when to suggest new products to individual customers. Kraft keeps a database on several million customers of Kraft products who request recipes, coupons, and other things from Kraft.

What is the right balance between working on customer acquisition versus customer retention?

Before a company starts to worry about acquiring new customers, it must develop a strategy to satisfy its existing customers. The key is to continuously invent new benefits for loyal customers; these might take the form of discounts, special invitations, or special reports and services. The company must give its sales force incentives to develop new business from its existing customers.

Any distribution of effort must take into account the cost of acquiring new customers, the cost of lost customers, customer lifetime value, and other factors.

What is multilevel marketing?

Multilevel marketing (also called network marketing) describes systems in which companies contract with individuals to sell a set of products door to door or office to office. It is called multilevel because a contractor can also invite others to work and earn money on their performance. Major multilevel companies include Amway and Avon, as well as hundreds of others selling jewelry or household products or vitamin programs. Multilevel marketing has provided part-time work opportunities to millions of people who can contact relatives, friends, and neighbors to sell products to them. Many multilevel companies essentially sell prospective workers the dream of becoming rich, and while some do become rich, many at best earn some extra income.

Internet Marketing

What kind of impact is the Internet having on marketing?

In the business-to-business area, the Internet is revolutionizing business practice and efficiency. Companies have much more information on suppliers and their prices, there is more reliance on auctions and requests for proposals, and many more transactions are taking place over the Net.

My guess is, however, that the average U.S. company is using only about 10 percent of the Internet's potential. Companies mistakenly believe that their Internet potential has been achieved when they open up a company web site. I would, however, ask the company the following questions:

- Do you use the Internet to test new product and marketing concepts using online focus groups and consumer panels?

- Have you assigned someone to research competitors' strategies, tactics, and resources on the Internet?
- Do you use the Internet to train and communicate with your employees, dealers, and suppliers?
- Do you use your web site to recruit new employees?
- Do you distribute coupons and product samples using your Web site?
- Do you monitor chat room conversations to learn how people talk about products, companies, and brands related to your business?

I suspect that most companies would not answer yes to many of these questions.

What are the characteristics of a good web site for a company?

Every company should design a web site that expresses the company's purpose, history, products, vision, and several other things. The web site should feature an easy way for the company to be contacted. It should feature new content on a continuous basis so that viewers will want to return to it. It should load onto the screen quickly, with interesting graphics. The web site may go beyond offering content to enabling transactions, which would make it an e-commerce site.

What are the limitations of buying goods via the Internet?

Buyers cannot feel or inspect the goods before purchase (although they can return them if they are dissatisfied). Buyers have to wait for the goods to be delivered (sometimes only two days), whereas they could normally acquire many products the same day at retail. Buyers can talk to someone face to face in a store, but this is not possible over the Internet, except in chat rooms or over the phone. Eventually buyers will be able to see salespeople on their computer screens, however.

Many online companies went bust. Why?

New online firms usually have good ideas to meet some latent needs in the marketplace. But although many online entrepreneurs are smart technically, they often lack marketing and financial skills. They fail to build a good business model. Here are the main reasons why many online companies went bust:

- Many online entrepreneurs rushed into the market without proper research or planning. They were bent on acquiring new customers, believing that the first company entering a category would capture category leadership.
- To acquire customers, online entrepreneurs spent large amounts on mass marketing and offline advertising to broadcast their name and business. They should have relied more on target marketing and viral marketing.
- They devoted too much effort to acquiring customers instead of building loyal and more frequent users among their present customers.
- They didn't really understand customer behavior when it comes to online surfing and purchasing.
- Many web sites were poorly designed, with problems of complexity, poor navigation, and downtime.
- Many online company web sites lacked adequate back-end infrastructures for shipping on time and for answering customer inquiries in a timely manner.
- Many web sites did not build a sound business model that would deliver eventual profits.
- The ease with which customers could switch web sites

in search of better prices forced e-commerce web sites to set margin-killing low prices.

At the same time, several online company web sites—such as eBay, Amazon, and Google—have been successful.

How has the Internet affected the relative importance of each of the 4Ps?

Price is becoming more important. A buyer is only a click away from comparing the prices charged by competitors for the same item. Promotion, in the case of advertising, is much less effective on the Internet. But sales promotion may be more effective because one can go to sites that offer free coupons for popular products (see Cool Savings or NetBonus). As for place, some retailers—those selling books, music, travel arrangement, and stock purchases—will be hurt by the Internet.

Professional Service Marketing

What can a professional service firm (PSF) do to better market itself?

First, a PSF, especially a smaller one, can do much better if it focuses and develops a leading reputation in one or a few areas rather than striving for a broad reputation in many areas. The head of an architecture firm told me that his firm could build any type of building. I said, "Suppose I want to build a hospital. Can you do a good job?" "Yes." I then asked, "But what if another firm has built many hospitals that are well-regarded? What can you do to convince the customer that you are more skilled at building hospitals?" He had no answer.

Second, a PSF should periodically measure client satisfaction. The firm should learn whether its fees are considered appropriate, that its professionals are respected and easy to reach, and so on.

Third, a PSF should develop a marketing planning process that sets long-range objectives from which the current plan can be drawn and the results measured over time. There should be a clear statement about where the firm wants to be in (say) five years and a credible strategy for getting there.

What are the biggest challenges facing professional service firms?

One major challenge is that PSFs are seen as pricing excessively for the services rendered. PSFs must do a better job of documenting their work time, and also documenting that they did the work in the most efficient manner. I know of a law firm that is willing to propose the cost of the work in advance, and if it is off the mark, it will absorb the difference. Clients want to know what the cost is likely to be.

Another challenge is the lack of brand differentiation among PSFs, even after a lot of advertising and brochure distribution. Firms need to project a clear set of values and competencies, and a distinct personality that differentiates them from their competitors.

What are your views on the need for professional service firms to hire sales personnel to get engagements?

Much depends on the type of PSF. Sales personnel would not be very effective in selling corporate law, for example. A client would want to personally interview the person or team that will do its legal work. In contrast, in accounting services, salespeople can be effective in getting accounts because accounting services are more standardized and do not depend on the brilliant accountant. In management consulting, strategic services will be bought directly through interviewing competing consulting firms, but there are some routine consulting services that can be sold by salespeople.

Personal Marketing

Do you think that in social relationships (like friendship and marriage), "personal marketing" is an effective tool to use?

Marketing does operate in social relationships, either consciously or unconsciously. Suppose a single man wants to meet a single woman and clicks on a dating service on the Internet. A major function of a market is to match buyers and sellers. Suppose the man identifies a woman to whom he is attracted. He will go into a "courtship" mode, which is a form of marketing. He will display his best side, a side that would please the woman. To that extent, the aim of marketing is to please both the buyer and the seller. After they marry, the question is whether he fulfills her expectations. Good marketing is about setting up expectations and fulfilling them; otherwise you have an unhappy customer, and sooner or later the relationship ends.

Can marketing be used to market *people* better?

A person can be seen as a brand. Certainly Madonna, Michael Jordan, and Jim Carrey are brands. A brand is a set of associations that we have about a product or a person. To that extent, people can try to design and manage their brand, that is, manage what they communicate about themselves to others. They may want to cultivate a creative persona or a tough persona or a caring persona, because somehow they feel that this will help them achieve their objectives. Celebrities and would-be-celebrities solicit the services of agents and public relations firms. These advisers often suggest changes in the person's activities, behavior, or attitudes that will improve his chances of achieving more visibility. I treated this topic in my coauthored book with Irving Rein called *High Visibility: The Making and Marketing of Professionals into Celebrities.*

Marketing cannot turn any person at random into a celebrity. A physicist is not going to win a Nobel prize by marketing herself. The physicist increases her chances mainly by defining important problems, doing the research, and creating breakthrough knowledge.

International Marketing

According to marketing theory, a company should adapt its offering to the host country. But others argue that a company should standardize its offering. What is your opinion on the matter?

Certain products are easy to sell in a standard form anywhere in the world. Examples include Coca-Cola, cameras, electronics, and so on. A Nikon digital camera can sell almost anywhere without product adaptation.

Other products, such as furniture, clothing, shoes, and food products, may require major local adaptation. Food products such as soup probably require flavor, packaging, and communication adjustments for different markets.

I remember a furniture company that tried to sell its furniture in another country without any design change. Two sales vice presidents were fired—in succession—because they couldn't sell the furniture. But the furniture had no appeal in that country.

Just because teenagers around the world may listen to similar music and all want Sony Playstations does not presage the disappearance of cultural enclaves. The first task of any global marketer is to get into the mindset of the people in that country. Then you won't start your meeting with a Mexican businessperson by talking about business, and you won't greet a Saudi Arabian businessperson by asking about his wife. One of the pleasures of the planet is the existence of different cultures.

A company needs to conduct an audit of local preferences and conditions and then change those elements—style, features, advertising, sales promotion, prices—that are warranted, provided that there is still a profit to be made.

How can a local company compete with global companies?

Local companies have to exploit their major advantage: They know the local market better. They know the language, laws, and buyer behavior and preferences better than global competitors. They can often spot limitations or weaknesses in the offers or practices of these global competitors. They often can price lower because they don't have the heavy management costs of the global company. The one problem might be that the local company must establish a reputation for high product and service quality. Otherwise the local company cannot compete against global competitors who deliver higher value to the local marketplace.

The hope for many developing companies is said to be export promotion. But how can a country figure out what its best exportable products are?

In *The Marketing of Nations*, I recommend that a nation assess its major strengths and weaknesses, and its major opportunities and threats (SWOT analysis). This will reveal those industries in which the country has a chance to achieve regional or global market share. Whether the answer is sugar, bananas, or colorful textiles, the next step is to create a brand-building strategy with the help of skilled advertising and public relations experts, and even government assistance. If the right image for the country's export products is developed and sufficient money is spent for repetition and variation of the message, the product could achieve export prominence.

How should companies organize themselves for global marketing? Should they be highly centralized or decentralized?

I like to think that all markets are local and that local managers know their local markets best. If their pay depends on their profit performance in the local market, they will normally do the right things for the local market. However, this is frustrating to product managers at headquarters, who think that their products deserve more attention in a local market than the country or local manager is providing. Companies will always face this dilemma: how much power to give local managers versus global product managers.

What role is played by a country's image in helping or hurting the sales of its products?

All countries have images that affect their foreign trade success for better or worse. We would not want to buy a jet airliner made in Borneo or take a holiday vacation in Iraq. When countries find that their current image is a handicap, they need to take steps to correct it, especially if it is not accurate or no longer accurate. Changing a country's image is time-consuming and costly. The task requires creative thinking about the country's strong points and how to communicate them. Nation "brand building" must be sustained over a long period of time.

Are the best marketing companies found only in the West?

Every country has a mix of smart and poor marketing companies. I would never say that most U.S. companies are practicing marketing in the right way. I find in every country a few stellar marketing performers. Some countries may put a certain stamp and style on their marketing. Companies from Japan and Switzerland typically emphasize high quality. Companies from China and Mexico emphasize low cost.

Isn't going abroad risky for a company?

Although going abroad is full of risks, domestic companies face even greater risks from the invasion of lower-price, higher-quality products from abroad. Companies should venture abroad, but they should avoid the following main causes of failure:

- Failure to take enough time to study the new market
- Failure to get reliable statistical information about the new market
- Failure to define the target user
- Failure to adapt the product and/or the marketing mix

- Failure to offer adequate service
- Failure to find good strategic partners

How have American companies handled their international operations?

In the early days, American companies handled their international operations by setting up an export department or an international division. More recently, companies such as Procter & Gamble have created regional companies. There is Procter & Gamble Europe, Procter & Gamble Asia, and so on. This enables companies to regionalize and localize their offerings instead of trying to sell identical products everywhere. At the same time, the regional arrangements are linked together with common strategies and shared platforms for manufacturing, procurement and distribution. I like ABB's motto: "A global company local everywhere."

Modern marketing has, by and large, been shaped by American marketing theory and practice. But aren't there different views of marketing in different countries?

I noticed a difference in how marketers abroad think of marketing. When I lecture in France, the marketing managers are most appreciative of elegant theory, even if it isn't very useful. German managers greatly respect theory but want it to be practical as well. British managers basically wanted practical tips and magic bullets for selling more stuff to more people.

In lecturing to the Japanese, I find that they literally accept the chief maxims of modern marketing, namely "know the customer" and "give the customer high value for the money." They would take down every word that I said as if it were gospel. My American students would be much more casual, as if they would learn the "real marketing" on the job. In 1980, I was upbraided by a CEO who said that I caused America's losses to the Japanese by teaching the Japanese to give better value for the money. I answered by saying that I taught that to everyone, but perhaps the Japanese listened.

Developing nations have attracted many multinationals to their shores. The multinationals can hurt many local businesses. Are they a blessing or a curse? How can local companies respond?

Multinationals that enter a country are a long-run blessing but a short-run curse. They are a long-run blessing in that they raise product and service quality and train a great number of the nation's people to be better managers and workers. A country should not lock out foreign competition. Brazil lost ten years of progress a few decades ago when it shut out foreign firms and decided to make its own computers and machinery; so much of it was inferior that Brazil couldn't sell its products abroad.

As for the short-run curse, each domestic company must study its multinational competitors. It will discover that they have some weaknesses, such as inflexibility, slow response time, not understanding the local consumer, or pricing too high for the market. Many multinationals focus on the up-scale market and thus miss the largest market group in a developing economy.

Local companies must benchmark their practices against the best ones found not only in their own country but abroad. Their business leaders should make regular trips to visit excellent companies abroad to learn from them. I have seen business leaders from Central and South America visit such companies as Federal Express, Disney, 3M, Hewlett-Packard, and L.L. Bean, and in each case take home great new marketing ideas.

What marketing approaches do multinational companies adopt when entering and selling in developing countries?

Multinationals entering developing countries have generally aimed their brands at the middle- and upper-class income levels. They succeeded initially because their products were better and were much preferred over local goods. Few multi-nationals bothered to make lower-cost brands for the mass market. India at one time almost passed a law saying that any multinational that introduced an expensive brand also had to introduce a less expensive brand for the masses. I feel that multinationals have missed an opportunity by not offer-ing lower-cost brands for the mass public in these countries. This need has been filled by local companies, and some have run circles around the multinationals by making goods that delivered better value to the people.

We are now seeing mega-retailers such as Wal-Mart and Carrefours bringing much lower prices to the citizens of these developing countries. I visited a new Wal-Mart in Beijing, and it was one of the busiest stores I have ever seen, with thousands of Chinese shoppers there daily. The major downside of these mega-retailers is that they are crushing small retailers and creating mass unemployment in the proc-ess. This may lead to increased pressure for protective legis-lation limiting the incursion of mega-retailers.

International trade is changing. Firms are becoming in-volved in global chains of production. What are the im-pacts of this business integration on marketing?

Businesses used to operate alone and negotiate temporary re-lationships that would benefit them. Today more businesses are involved in business networks and partnerships. Large companies are attempting to build frictionless value-delivery systems that include many partners. Each local business has to figure out with whom it should ally. If a business avoids alliances, it may lose out entirely; if it allies with poor partners, it will also lose out. Businesses must exercise good judgment as to which alliances to pursue.

In the new business landscape, China poses a strong economic challenge to other countries. From a marketing perspective, how should countries respond to such a seemingly unbeatable challenge?

China will inevitably become the world's largest economy. As China's economy grows, it will need inputs of various kinds: steel, building materials, electronics, water treatment, schools, and many other things. It can source some of these inputs internally, but it will need to source many of them externally. Therefore companies have to think through China's growth trajectory and figure out where their core competencies and product lines can fit in profitably. China's rapid growth has resparked the growth of companies in Asia who can sell their supplies to China.

Place Marketing

Can the United States be marketed? If so, how?

The United States is marketed everywhere everyday, for good or bad, by McDonald's, Coca-Cola, and Hollywood. It advertises its brand of capitalism as one of free markets, free trade, and freedom of the press. It attracts admiration, it attracts envy, and it attracts censure for many of its ways and outcomes. People abroad have different social and economic philosophies, outlooks, and experiences, and these color their attitudes. Therefore, when a nation, such as the United States, tries to transmit a specific identity to the rest of the world, its image is bound to be distorted and refracted by people's experience and political and social leanings.

I think the United States needs a fresh marketing program that drops some of the old rhetoric and presents a new view of universal values and aspirations, not limited to the seeming cowboy mentality that some of its leaders project. Any campaign would have to be preceded by real changes in foreign policy and deeds.

How difficult is it for a nation to alter its image?

Very difficult. It is unlikely that any well-known nation can do much to alter its image radically. But it can correct some minor problems in its image. For example, the French government under Mendes-France was not happy with the way French merchants treated American tourists. They were somewhat haughty and distant. So he pushed a campaign to convince French merchants that it was in their interest to be more welcoming and friendly to American tourists. This campaign eventually changed French attitudes, and the change was perceived by American visitors to France.

Who is really in the business of nation branding: governments, business leaders, or both?

Both! Suppose Ireland wants to attract tourists. The Irish Tourist Bureau (a government organization) will have primary responsibility for developing Ireland's image as a tourist destination. But it will work closely with hotels, airlines, and restaurants to gain concurrence on the images to be used to sell tourists on vacationing in Ireland.

And if Ireland wants to attract companies to build their

factories in Ireland, this responsibility is placed in the hands of the Irish Development Agency (IDA). Presumably the government has defined a long-run economic development plan identifying the types of industries that Ireland wants to attract. The Irish Development Agency would work up the brand rhetoric to show that Ireland is a very favorable place to locate production in terms of taxes, worker quality and costs, property availability, and infrastructure. The IDA would work with local companies and national trade associations to carry out the work of enticing companies to choose Ireland for their investments.

The most successful cases of nation branding (and city and region branding) involve a true partnership between the public and private sectors. The public sector cannot accomplish much on its own. If it developed and circulated a brand identity on its own, the private sector might not live up to it or deliver on it. Furthermore, drawing in the private sector has the advantage of providing more "arms" to multiply the diffusion of any agreed-upon place image.

Place marketing is quite new, having received its theoretical sendoff with *Marketing Places* and *The Marketing of Nations*. Subsequently my coauthors and I prepared *Marketing Places Europe*, *Marketing Asian Places*, and *Marketing Place in Latin America and the Caribbean*. Before that, a few marketing scholars had worked on "country-of-origin" studies designed to measure the effect of a country's image on product and brand perceptions and preferences. However, these studies did not go into how a nation might improve its branding.

What are the biggest marketing obstacles facing post-communist countries?

Different postcommunist countries are making the transition at different rates, depending upon a number of factors.

Countries that had an industrial history before communism have a better chance than countries that were largely agricultural. Countries that are moving faster to dismantle state enterprises and put them into the hands of competent multinationals have a better chance of improving faster. Countries that have a better educational system and that have been building business schools (not just economics programs) have a better chance. And countries with a more entrepreneurial mentality have a better chance.

Even when good ideas abound, the big obstacle in post-communist countries is funding. There is a need for forward-looking financial institutions that will lend money to worthwhile enterprises and start-ups. One welcome development would be the emergence of strong venture capital firms willing to accept risk in exchange for equity.

Recession Marketing

What policies and strategies make sense for companies during an economic recession?

When a recession occurs, a company often rushes to cut its expenses, especially its marketing expenditures, and reduce its prices. It would be smart if, instead of this, the company appointed a multidepartmental committee to propose what it should do to reduce costs. With respect to marketing costs, the committee should examine the company's promotion mix, channel mix, market segment mix, customer mix, and geographical mix to identify activities and expenses that could safely be reduced. Every company has some losing or weak *advertising, promotions, channels, market segments, customers,* and *geographical areas.* A recession calls for housecleaning.

Companies can save money by switching their salespeople to economy-class flights and hotels, or by doing more business by phone and e-mail. Companies can try to renegotiate purchase contracts. They can delay selected long-term R&D projects and postpone capital projects. They can try to speed up collections and slow down payments.

During a recession, customers are looking for lower prices or more value for their money. A company should consider introducing a second line of lower-cost products and also make greater use of sales promotion (e.g., cents-off promotions, rebates, or coupons) as opposed to actually cutting the list price.

Business-to-business companies should work closely with their customers to find ways to reduce customer costs, not necessarily through price reductions, but through better ways to utilize the company's products or operate the customer's business.

In the flurry to do this, a company should remember three things. Don't cut expenses where this would hurt the brand's value proposition, which has taken so long to build. Instead of rushing to cut prices, focus on ways to increase the value delivered to the customer. And finally, some companies might use the recession to launch aggressive marketing to attract customers away from competitors.

Political Marketing

Do you think that marketing professionals can help politicians win elections?

Politicians have always marketed and been marketed. They hunt for headlines, kiss babies, attend endless coffee parties, and hire advertising agencies to shape their image. Today, political marketers advise candidates what to wear, where to speak, what to say (and not say), whom to be seen with, and so on. A candidate's every public move is scripted, much as a product's packaging and shelf position are fine-tuned. I don't know how this can be curbed or avoided. Presumably, in a democratic system with more than one political party, each party is doing this, and there is some cancellation of effects. However, the real worry is that the election will go to the party with the bigger marketing budget, not the better candidate.

Do marketers feel any ethical conflict in "selling" the image of political candidates?

Marketers face ethical questions all the time. I have refused to help companies market tobacco products or guns. Yet some other marketers who believe in the rights of people to smoke or carry guns will feel that helping these companies is very ethical. And if I believed in the quality of a particular political candidate, I would have no qualms about marketing this person. Yet many political marketers sell their services to market any candidate, whether or not they believe in that candidate, in much the same way that a lawyer will take on either side of any case, whether or not she believes in its merits.

Social Responsibility Marketing

The economist Milton Friedman famously said: "There is one and only one social responsibility of business—to use its resources and engage in activities designed to increase its profits." What are your thoughts on the social responsibility of marketing?

In the 1970s, I began to distinguish between business marketing, nonprofit marketing, social marketing, and societal marketing. We know what *business marketing* is. *Nonprofit marketing* describes the efforts of nonprofit organizations to attract clients and funds to support social and cultural services such as aid to the needy, museums and theatrical performances, and public health initiatives. I formulated *social marketing* as a discipline for trying to influence healthy behavior (e.g., healthy eating and daily exercise) and discourage unhealthy behavior (e.g., smoking or using hard drugs). *Societal marketing* focuses on the impact that marketing practices have on the well-being of society. In this case, I said that companies should distinguish between satisfying a person's needs, weighing the impact on the person's well-being, and the impact on the public's well-being. Thus smoking a cigarette meets the person's need, but it hurts his health and it increases the public's health costs.

The scandals involving Enron, WorldCom, Tyco, and other companies have damaged the reputation of companies and created public suspicion of Big Business. There is a feeling that many companies "sail very close to the wind," but stay on just the right side of the law and/or the moral issue (or at least are not found out). When all is said, companies are under pressure to set and practice higher standards of business behavior.

Companies within the same industry are losing differentiation. One remaining way for consumers to choose among competitors is to pay attention to the company's civic character. The public likes to buy from companies that "care" as long as there are no major differences in their products, quality, or prices.

Finally, I would argue that companies benefit greatly from the health of the surrounding society. They are, in turn, obligated to contribute to the health of the surrounding society through good deeds.

Nancy Lee and I published *Corporate Social Responsibility* to help companies answer such questions as: Are we now giving anything back to society? How much should we give back? What social investment would create the most good for the company and the social cause? How can we measure the impact of our contributions on the recipients and on our own reputation?

What is the case for morality in marketing?

I believe that ethical companies will outperform unethical companies in the long run. A company that is desperate enough to cut corners to reach its profit goals is behaving foolishly and putting its stockholders' money at risk. As a stockholder, I would rather accept lower performance and a slight drop in stock price than see the company's management risk a huge drop in stock value as a result of a scandal. I favor sending managers to jail who mismanage through ethical and legal lapses. I also favor rewarding whistle-blowers who expose corrupt business practices within their companies. The answer to making long-run profits is continuous improvement and innovating to provide new streams of value to your customers, not fudging the numbers.

I have been urging companies to exhibit more social responsibility and ethical behavior. We judge companies by the quality of their products, the promptness with which they resolve customer issues, and the degree of fairness they show. Companies today are being rated on their ethics, and there are mutual funds that invest only in socially responsible companies. We should judge companies by their deeds more than by their statements. Do they give money to charity? Do they support some worthwhile causes? Are their operations transparent? Even their deeds can sometimes fool us, however. Enron gave millions of dollars to charity, and behind this was an "evil empire."

Do you believe that consumers need government protection?

I am generally in favor of both the government and nongovernmental consumer groups acting to protect and educate consumers. Consumers cannot be expected to know what drugs, foods, and products are safe. A side benefit is that regulation also protects good companies from the assault of bad companies. Therefore, ethical companies should also be in favor of consumer protection.

Company decisions have an impact on society as well as on individuals. Can you distinguish between the types of impact?

Companies need to consider the impact of their activities on society. There are three levels that can be distinguished. First, does our product satisfy the customer? Second, is our product good for the customer? Third, is our product good for the society? Take the example of cigarettes. Cigarettes satisfy the smoker. However, they are not good for the customer. And finally, they hurt society because the society has to bear much higher medical costs. Take another example, the Hummer automobile, which gets only ten miles per gallon of gas. The owner enjoys the Hummer, and it doesn't harm the owner. But it does harm society because it pollutes the environment and makes the society more dependent on imports of oil.

What are a company's social responsibilities? Does greater social responsibility lead to greater profits?

Every company should consider two matters: its business ethics and its corporate social responsibility. Business ethics focuses on the behavior of the company's employees. Corporate social responsibility focuses on the contributions that the company can make to worthwhile social causes. Both are important, and some companies have appointed two high-level officers to be responsible for these two functions. Ultimately, these functions are the responsibility of the CEO and the company's board.

How can managers in newly industrializing countries learn about ethics and social responsibility?

I would advise that professional groups in developing countries—brokers, analysts, financial advisers, bankers—contact their corresponding trade or professional associations in the United States or Western Europe to collect the codes of their profession. These codes should serve as the basis for hammering out an appropriate code for the industrializing country. The codes should include a penalty mechanism for punishing deviant practitioners. Every society has a certain number of flagrant operators who are capable of giving their company or their industry a bad name. And there are always gullible consumers eager to partake in "get-rich-quick" schemes who ultimately are hurt. This problem will never be eliminated; it is present everywhere, and yet we must do our best to create a regulatory system to curtail it and a literate population that is wise in matters of spending, investing, and saving.

What is social marketing?

Social marketing encompasses efforts to change public behavior in directions that are deemed desirable by society. Most societies regard drunkenness, drug abuse, littering, and certain other behaviors as both individually and socially undesirable. Social marketing is the application of marketing techniques to increase adoption of high-consensus ideas and causes. Social marketers influence positive change through the use of incentives, facilitation, and promotion.

What gave you the initial impetus to develop social marketing? And how has the field developed?

I always had a passionate interest in social action to address social problems. In the early 1970s, I began to sense that marketing had a powerful set of concepts and tools that could help social action groups make some headway in addressing social problems. I had already written an article with Sidney Levy in 1969 called "Broadening the Concept of Marketing," in which we argued that marketing is not limited to commercial markets but can be of use in the work of nonprofit and government organizations.

In 1970, I was approached by a number of social action groups for help with such issues as family planning, environmental pollution, and poverty. I suggested to Gerald Zaltman, who was interested in the same issues, that we write an article to show how social action groups could be more effective by segmenting markets and understanding better the mindsets and behavior of consumers.

We saw social marketing as an alternative to coercion or legal action in solving social problems. We also thought that education was too slow an approach to produce desirable changes in behavior. We hoped that social marketing would provide a more proactive and powerful set of tools for social action, aiming to create voluntary changes in behavior based on benefits exchanged.

In *Social Marketing: Improving the Quality of Life,* Nancy Lee, Ned Roberto, and I described more than one hundred examples of successful social marketing campaigns. We also noted the large number of social marketing researchers, the establishment of the Social Marketing Institute, the recognition of social marketing by major global and health organizations, the existence of major university research centers focusing on social marketing, and other signs of progress. I am pleased to see a lively social marketing scene in the new millennium.

What needs to be done to recruit more marketing students and marketing professionals into the field of social marketing?

Social marketing needs to be marketed to major social action groups, both governmental and nongovernmental, so that these groups will seek more social marketing consultants and offer more funding for social marketing campaigns. This will convince marketing students and marketing professionals that they can find a challenging and remunerative career in social marketing.

Many health professionals have embraced social marketing, but far too many still equate social marketing with the use of media campaigns and fancy messages to persuade consumers to change their behavior. How can we do a better job of distinguishing between health communication and social marketing?

Social marketing is a larger idea than social promotion and advertising. We need to highlight the importance of the other three Ps, product, price, and place, in determining whether a social marketing campaign will be successful. We must add the idea that client behavior analysis, segmentation, and positioning are critical concepts in developing our social marketing approach.

Is Green Marketing an important part of marketing?

The amount of attention given to Green Marketing is dictated by the severity of the country's environmental problems, the strength of green activist groups, the amount of newspaper coverage and agitation, the amount of cleanup money available, and international pressures. Most companies will do nothing unless laws are passed. Some companies call themselves green marketers without doing much about it. A few companies, however, will see authentic business opportunities in taking leadership in green marketing and will win valuable public confidence. These green-marketing leaders will think in long-run terms and take a holistic view of the value-creation process. Sooner or later, businesses must factor environmental concerns into their planning and operations. Individual firms are not likely to do this on their own, because it will raise their costs and hurt their competitiveness. The hope is that industry associations will set standards. Otherwise the government will have to impose environmental requirements on entire industries.

PART 8

Marketing Excellence

What companies best exemplify excellent marketing?

My favorite companies based on their innovative marketing strategies are:

IKEA	Starbucks
Southwest Airlines	Sony
Wal-Mart	Virgin
Amazon.com	Ben & Jerry
Dell Computer	The Body Shop
Toyota	Harley Davidson
Enterprise Rent-A-Car	Nike
Progressive Insurance	Absolut Vodka
USAA Insurance	Amway
Barnes & Noble	eBay.com
Charles Schwab	Disney
FedEx	Swatch watches

A rich story can be told about how each of these companies invented a new way of doing business in its industry. Some of them dramatically reduced customers' costs (IKEA, Southwest Airlines, Wal-Mart, Enterprise Rent-a-Car). Some of them dramatically improved product quality or customer experience (Starbucks, Sony, Toyota). Others reinvented the nature of the business (Barnes & Noble, Charles Schwab, FedEx).

At the same time, we must recognize that some favorites don't last. I am less excited now by previous strong innovators such as Rubbermaid, Saturn, Benetton, and Club Mediterranee, among others.

Furthermore, I would include a list of my favorite marketing thinkers:

Walt Disney of The Walt Disney Company

Ray Kroc of McDonald's

Roberto Goizueta of Coca-Cola

Howard Schultz of Starbucks

Ingvar Kamprad of IKEA

Sam Walton of Wal-Mart

Richard Branson of Virgin

What about examples of what not to do?

Two landmark disaster cases are the Edsel and New Coke. Ford designed the Edsel to meet its own need for a product sandwiched between Fords and Lincolns. But the public didn't need it! Furthermore, it ended up looking as if one team had designed the front end and another team had designed the back end, without talking to each other. The New Coke fiasco amounted to Coca-Cola's tampering with its age-old formula without recognizing the wishes of millions of Coke lovers who wanted it to stay the same.

When you go to the doctor for a checkup, he performs a routine to make sure you're OK. What basic marketing checkup steps would you perform on a company to get a sense of its marketing health?

Tom Peters once said that you can go into a store or office and tell in fifteen minutes whether it is alive or dead. In my case, I score a company on how well it has applied my Ten Commandments for Marketing Success (see *The Ten Deadly Sins of Marketing: Signs and Solutions*).

1. The firm segments the market, chooses the best segments, and develops a strong position in each segment.
2. The firm maps customers' needs, perceptions, preferences, and behavior and motivates its stakeholders to obsess about serving and satisfying the customers.
3. The firm knows its major competitors and their strengths and weaknesses.
4. The firm has made partners out of its key stakeholders (employees, suppliers, distributors) and generously rewards them.
5. The firm develops systems for identifying opportunities, ranking them, and choosing the best ones.
6. The firm manages a marketing planning system that leads to insightful long-term and short-term plans.
7. The firm exercises strong control over its product and service mix.
8. The firm builds strong brands by using the most cost-effective communication and promotion tools.
9. The firm builds marketing leadership and a team spirit among its various departments.
10. The firm constantly adds technology that will give it a competitive advantage in the marketplace.

Can any company dominate a market for very long?

Companies will try to dominate markets, but they are naïve in thinking that they will succeed on a permanent basis. Market domination is temporary, and the high profits of one firm will attract market disrupters. Short of state-protected monopolies or property rights monopolies, most market domination will be short-lived.

Most companies don't last very long. A few do. What are the secrets?

The average large company has an expected life of twenty years. It is much less for small businesses. Company mortality is the result of a company's not changing with the times, being acquired by another company, being hit by unexpected financial difficulties, and so on. However, some companies have lasted hundreds of years. Among them are Royal Dutch/Shell, Dupont, W. R. Grace, Kodak, Mitsui, Sumitomo, and Unilever. The question of what accounts for some companies thriving over an extended time period has been addressed in two excellent books:

- James Collins, *Built to Last* (and his recent book, *Good to Great*)
- Arie De Geus, *The Living Company*

Can you describe a few innovative companies in more detail?

I'll describe IKEA and Calyx & Corolla as two separate examples.

IKEA fits my description of a great value-adding company. Ingvar Kamprad was pained about the high costs of furniture facing young people in Sweden who were setting up households for the first time. He worked hard to drive down the cost of making and selling furniture, emphasizing the cost savings of knockdown furniture and the advantages of mass production and marketing. But he did more than create high-quality affordable furniture. He added features to the IKEA experience that showed a sensitivity to how people shop for furniture. He added a restaurant, recognizing that furniture shopping takes a long time and people get hungry. He added a day-care center, recognizing that children become difficult during long shopping trips and are better separated from their parents while they are focusing on the goods. He built loyalty by introducing a membership program and lower prices on many goods for members. I would nominate IKEA as a company belonging in the Marketing Hall of Fame.

Calyx & Corolla provides an interesting case of innovative thinking. The firm's founder, Ruth M. Owades, recognized that flowers travel through the labyrinth of wholesalers and retailers for almost ten days between the time they are grown and the time they reach customers. She set up a system of direct marketing to homes. Customers can order fresh flowers and bouquets from her catalog, from her web page, or by phone. The order is immediately sent electronically to one of twenty-five growers in her network, who pick and package the flowers and ship them via FedEx. They arrive fresh, last ten days longer, and satisfy many consumers.

Can you give an example of companies that interact well with their customers?

Smart firms build *customer communities*. Harley-Davidson, manufacturer of the famous brand of motorcycles, has created over 300,000 loyal fans. They not only adore the company but also like to meet each other. Brand communities are easier to build around products that are major purchases, such as cars, motorcycles, or Apple computers. The other solution is to work with customers one-to-one. The USAA insurance company does all of its business over the telephone (and more recently over the Internet). Although there are no face-to-face meetings with customers, their customers love the firm. The telephone salespeople are superb and almost sound like friends talking to friends.

Can you name a company in an emerging country that has shown exceptional sophistication?

I have seen some companies in emerging countries that perform better than their counterparts in advanced industrial countries. The Amil health insurance company of Brazil is one of the best value-adding companies I have seen. It not only sells health insurance but mentors its customers on healthier lifestyles by supplying them with health literature, helping them stop smoking, and so on. The same plaudits go to another Brazilian company, HSM, the seminar firm, which is setting world-class standards on running management training programs around the world (for details, see pp. 153–155 of *Kotler on Marketing*).

Can you name some European companies and researchers that have been innovative?

We can cite examples from every country. Let me confine the answer to Sweden. I have been impressed with the marketing innovations of several Swedish companies. SAS airlines, under Jan Carlson, introduced the "moments of truth" idea that became a platform for further service innovation. Volvo illustrated the power of a company that focuses on a major desired benefit, namely, safe automobiles. IKEA showed how cost can be driven down in a traditional industry, namely, furniture retailing. Ericsson has contributed to our ideas on innovation, and Electrolux to our practice of brand management. Many other Swedish companies could also be cited.

Swedish academics have been prominent in creating new marketing perspectives. Evert Gummesson of Stockholm University has profoundly advanced our understanding of relationship marketing and service marketing. Lars-Gunnar Mattson has pioneered the study of business networks. In fact, Swedish academics have been instrumental in moving our focus away from a narrow concentration on mass marketing of consumer packaged goods to larger issues of business-to-business relationships and networks.

What is the biggest marketing strength of American companies? What is their biggest weakness?

The biggest marketing strengths of American companies are their competitive culture and cost discipline. The biggest weakness of American companies is the short-run performance horizon needed to please their impatient stockholders. The pressure for a short-term response is intense, especially in publicly traded companies, which base their decisions on how those decisions will affect the company's current stock price. I have always believed that privately held companies have much more freedom to make the right long-term decisions. "Short-term" decisions usually come back to haunt the company.

What books would you recommend for a marketing manager (chief marketing officer of a medium or large company) who is trying to make his company more competitive?

There are many interesting and insightful books on marketing. I would recommend the following books, recognizing that there are many more dealing with specific topics:

1. Kevin Keller, *Strategic Brand Management* (or any of David Aaker's books on branding)
2. Fred Reichheld, *The Loyalty Effect* (or his book *Loyalty Rules!*)
3. Leonard Berry, *Discovering the Soul of Service* (or his book *On Great Service*)

4. Dawn Iacobucci, ed., *Kellogg on Marketing* (the best set of current essays on different subjects in marketing)
5. Roland T. Rust, et al. *Driving Customer Equity*
6. Don Peppers and Martha Rogers, *The One-to-One Future*

Each of these books started new thinking in marketing.

Do business books have an influence on how business is conducted?

Some business books offer new ideas that businesses put into practice. Among such influential books have been those by Peter Drucker, Tom Peters, W. Edwards Deming, Michael Porter, and Gary Hamel. Other business books describe what leading companies are already doing but bring these ideas to a larger audience.

What is the most important idea or person that has influenced your thinking on business?

Businesses are finally grasping the idea that winning companies choose segments and make them central to their strategy and operations. Customer focus is critical in a world that is no longer plagued by a shortage of goods but faces a shortage of customers. I have been deeply influenced by Peter Drucker, who observed decades ago that "marketing . . . is the whole business seen from the point of view of its final result, that is, from the customer's point of view." Drucker added, "A business has two—and only two—basic functions: *marketing* and *innovation*. Marketing and innovation produce results: all the rest are costs."

Index